BEATING the BUSINESS CYCLE

BEATING the BUSINESS CYCLE

How to Predict and Profit from Turning Points in the Economy

Lakshman Achuthan and Anirvan Banerji

Currency Doubleday

New York   London   Toronto   Sydney   Auckland

To the memory of Geoffrey H. Moore

A CURRENCY BOOK
Published by Doubleday
a division of Random House, Inc.

CURRENCY is a trademark of Random House, Inc., and
DOUBLEDAY is a registered trademark of Random House, Inc.

Book design by Erin L. Matherne and Tina Thompson

Cataloging-in-Publication Data is on file with the Library of Congress.

ISBN 0-385-50953-7

PRINTED IN THE UNITED STATES OF AMERICA

First Edition: June 2004

10 9 8 7 6 5 4 3 2 1

CONTENTS

ACKNOWLEDGMENTS

We are deeply indebted to our families for their affection and support during the many long evenings and weekends we spent writing this book—especially our wives, Tracy White and Aloka Banerji. They, along with Shelby White and Arup Banerji, helped us speak much more clearly than we would have on our own. We will always be grateful for the unwavering confidence and constant encouragement of our parents, Joy Mayfield, M. Radh Achuthan, Meena Banerji, and Amitav Banerji, in this, as in other endeavors. We miss Leon Levy, father-in-law and friend, whose encouragement and insights into human behavior were always offered with playful wit.

We could not have written this book without the help of our friends and colleagues at ECRI, particularly Philip Klein, Lorene Hiris, Allan Layton, Pami Dua, Jean Maltz, Dimitra Visviki, Mi-Suk Ha, Hui-Chun Jan, Eleni Constaninou, Julienne Kim, and Deepika Gupta, who helped create most of the fine charts that are critical to the story we tell. We will never forget Jack Cullity, whose research collaboration and friendship we miss dearly.

Our friend Victor Neary first persuaded us to write this book, and introduced us to Al Lowman, whose vision took us straight to Doubleday. The fine people who work there deserve much credit for this book—particularly our editor, Roger Scholl, and his colleague, Sarah Rainone, who worked tirelessly to help us prepare it for publication.

In addition, we are thankful to Keith Hollihan for his invaluable help in shaping the structure of our writing as we moved from an idea to words on paper.

Melita Moore has always offered us sound advice, and much of that is reflected in our writing. We are also in debt to Chuck Brunie and Peter Darling for their sage counsel and insightful comments on the book.

Finally, we are obliged to the many people we have met in the course of our working lives, for the conversations, questions, and shared insights that have both motivated and shaped this book.

PART ONE

 The Cyclical
Worldview

The Resurrection of Risk

In the Road Runner cartoon the joke is always the same. Wile E. Coyote chases the Road Runner, misses a sharp turn, and runs right over the edge of the cliff. He looks down and, realizing too late that he is in midair, plunges into the chasm below.

This may seem uncomfortably familiar to those who found themselves carried away by the excitement of the 1990s economic boom. Too late they realized that profits, jobs, or stock prices were already in a free fall. But, unlike the cartoon, it was not funny. A shift from boom to bust, from economic expansion to recession, like the one we experienced in 2001, can be painful, even tragic, for those blindsided by the downturn. That is why it is so critical to be forewarned of turning points in the economy.

Is that even possible? Many would say "no." It is true that economic forecasters rarely get recession calls right. In fact, as a recent study concluded, "The [worldwide] record of failure to predict recessions is virtually unblemished."[1]

But we are here to tell you a different story. It really *is* possible to predict recessions. And we will show you how, so that you will no longer be at the mercy of economic cycles. Whether you are an employee or a student, a business manager or a policy maker, you can learn to navigate the economy's ups and downs.

We will describe a cyclical framework for viewing the economy that relies on an array of objective indicators that, if used properly, warn of turning points *before* they happen. We will also tell you why many of the commonly followed economic indicators can be misleading. You'll discover you don't need a Ph.D. in economics or even a full-time focus on the economy to use our techniques.

But if recessions have historically been so hard to predict, why should you listen to us? Because we have accurately predicted recessions and recoveries when others have failed.[2]

We were able to do this not because we are smarter than other forecasters, or because we have some secret formula, but because at the Economic Cycle Research Institute (ECRI) an eighty-year tradition of business cycle research gives us a unique vantage point. By standing on the shoulders of the giants of business cycle research who pioneered our approach, we have, over time, designed objective tools that accurately predict turning points in the economy. In *Beating the Business Cycle,* we share this information so that you, too, can create your own customized "economic dashboard" that will help steer your future financial decisions in the right direction before you find yourself plunging into the abyss.

Our research tradition was handed down to us by Geoffrey H. Moore, the legendary business cycle scholar whom *The Wall Street Journal* called "the father of leading indicators." Moore was the protégé of Wesley C. Mitchell and Arthur F. Burns, who, early in the twentieth century, pioneered modern business cycle research. Moore's career spanned six decades and focused on the development of practical tools to monitor and predict economic cycles. His approach stands in stark contrast to the views of a generation of economic researchers who shrugged their shoulders long ago, resigned to the belief that forecasting turns in the cycle was impossible and therefore irrelevant. Moore founded the independent Economic Cycle Research Institute to advance the tradition of cyclical research, as well as to refine its predictive tools and make those results available to as many people as possible.

We believe these tools are invaluable in helping you make decisions about your business and your personal life. Why? Because there are both opportunities and dangers linked to the ups and downs of the business cycle that you need to know. When will the next turning point in the economy arrive? How can you avoid getting hurt in a bust? When can you capitalize on the opportunities a boom will offer? This book will give you those answers. It will help you to reduce the risk of being blindsided by an economic downturn and allow you to take full advantage of the good times. So while most economic books are liable to put you to sleep, this book should help you to sleep better.

Wile E. Coyote, after scraping himself off the canyon floor, again gives chase, heedless of the dangers ahead, oblivious to any lessons he might learn. Because he is only a cartoon character, no matter how many times he gets splattered, he never really gets hurt. But life is not a cartoon. And if you are the one to take a nosedive when the economy makes an unexpected turn, the pain is real. It may not be so easy to peel yourself off the canyon floor.

A DIFFERENT PERSPECTIVE

The 2001 recession was the first time many of us experienced what it feels like to go from a boom to a bust. The fact is, with forewarning, the pain could have been considerably less. But the din of the late-1990s euphoria was simply too loud for most people to hear any voice not in harmony with the boom-market revelry.

In September 2000, ECRI warned of a recession ahead[3] to our clients, and later on the evening news shows. Few listened. Most kept upping the ante, convincing themselves and one another that any economic rough spots were only minor speed bumps. It was easy to be swept along by the enthusiasm of the New Economy.

For much of the 1990s, it was worth joining in on the fun. Contrarians missed out on the longest expansion in U.S. history, as the stock market climbed from well below 4,000 to over 11,000. Clearly, during the boom, the important question was "When is it the right time to break away from the bulls?" And in the wake of a bust, it is just as important to know when to part company with the pessimists. The bottom of an economic cycle is the perfect time to ask, "Is now the time to add to my business by buying out competitors while prices are low?"

These questions are answerable. You need not live in a constant state of fear, wondering where the economy is headed. The tools we employ to forecast recessions and recoveries for our major clients can be used by any business or individual. The objective indicators we have developed will tell you when we are approaching a turning point in the economy. We will show you how to read them and use them when making different kinds of financial decisions. But you must be strong enough to trust them—especially when they cut against the grain of popular opinion. And believe us—at the most critical times, they will.

The research that gave rise to these indicators has too long been hidden from public view. Back in the 1920s and 1930s, there was a great deal of interest in business cycles as a result of the boom of the 1920s and the Great Depression that followed. But memories fade. Most forecasters have forgotten the work of Mitchell, Burns, and Moore. This is part of the reason so many economists and financial experts were blindsided by the 2001 recession, and why much of what you read here will seem new.

In March 2001, six months after we issued our initial warning of a recession, it became clear to us that a recession was unavoidable. We were not shy about saying so. *The New York Times* published our call on its front page.[4] In hindsight, it is agreed that was precisely when the recession began.[5]

We do not want to suggest that it was easy to make the call. Far from it. Over a decade had passed since our last recession call in February 1990, five months before the previous recession started. Because we are experts in business cycle forecasting and had the record to prove it, we were under enormous pressure. To make things even more stressful, this was the first recession forecast we would make without the help of Moore, who had passed away a year earlier. (Some believed that it was Moore's uncanny intuition about the direction of the economy that helped us make calls, rather than his research.) In spite of these challenges, we knew that our well-tested methods would steer us correctly. The entire ECRI staff gathered together, spending two weeks poring over each and every indicator. Only then did we steel ourselves to go public; we concluded that it would be irresponsible to do otherwise.

What led us to that conclusion? Not since the mid-1970s had the world's three largest economies—the United States, Japan, and Germany—contracted in sync. We saw that kind of synchronous contraction again in 2001. Nonetheless, for most of the year, few believed that the party was over. Confident that the economic boom would soon resume, the stock market rallied through late May—three months into the recession. Denial persisted even as corporate profits plunged and job losses mounted. In fact, cheerleaders of the boom economy continued their good-times refrain through September 10, 2001, even though stock prices had been dropping sharply since May.

By September 11, the recession was six months old. In the wake of the terrorist attacks, the confusion and the boost from emergency economic stimuli allowed some pundits to continue denying the reality of recession. Others blamed the economy's woes on the unpredictable shock of those attacks.

In the months that followed, many viewed the emerging corporate scandals at Enron, WorldCom, and Arthur Andersen, as well as the intensification of the Israeli-Palestinian conflict and the continued threat from al-Qaeda, as evidence of a "perfect storm" of freak events that caused the recession. Such a view implied that the storm would pass and things would return to the way they were. But the recession did not result from any such storm. In fact, it preceded it. Like earlier busts, it resulted from the wide gap between perceptions and reality, as the wishful thinking about an ever-expanding economy got a wake-up call from the business cycle.

The momentum of the late-1990s boom carried perceptions of growth forward, beyond the downturn that marked the onset of recession. Business managers planned for demand that suddenly vanished; individuals made important career or financial decisions based on a roaring economy; investors held on to large positions in stocks because they believed double-digit returns would continue. Few factored the risk of a recession into their plans, and when one hit with the force of a falling Acme safe, many people were left feeling like the flattened Coyote.

Why were so many caught off guard by the downturn? Certainly the cheerleaders of the New Economy were partly to blame, along with a general belief that the business cycle was dead. But the fundamental reason rests with human nature. When looking to the future, people naturally project from the recent past. Just like Wile E. Coyote, we think that because the road has been straight for some time, it will remain so.

As long as the economy is proceeding in the same general direction, you can easily adjust major business decisions, such as whether to expand your company, hire new employees, or implement cost-cutting measures; in your personal life, you can postpone or accelerate major decisions such as buying or selling a house or changing jobs. But as a turning point in the economy approaches, the gap between reality and one's expectations can lead to painful consequences, and you can find yourself quickly heading in the wrong direction.

During the downturn of 2001, many businesses and individuals experienced this devastation firsthand. The severity of the drop was worsened by the extent to which CEOs believed the hype that recessions were a thing of the past. The fiber-optics and telecom industries built up tremendous overcapacity as a result. Cisco Systems, for example, continued to order equipment from its vendors long after customer orders began to dry up. The bust, in effect, was ensured by the growing dismissal of risk, which led to reckless behavior.

When business leaders, the media, government officials, economists, and individuals make such mistakes together, things go wrong in a big way. A herd mentality takes over and otherwise sane and rational people do crazy things. This tendency lay at the foundation of the biggest stock market bust of our generation. The urge to believe that the future would be like the recent past, combined with a kind of mass euphoria, blinded people to the possibility that the economic times may change.

If bullish behavior during booms and bubbles feels rational at the time, so can pessimism and anxiety during downturns. Like it or not, our assessment of the future is colored by emotion. Subjective interpretations are driven by both the recent past and the prevailing wisdom, and will always lag at economic turning points. Although many people were hurt when the economy turned down, as time passes those scars, too, will fade, and caution will eventually again give way to complacency. When the next recession hits, most people, oblivious of the turn in the cycle, will make the same mistake as before. In the same way, we may, with the recent recession in mind, fail to take advantage of the next boom in the economy. To break from this pattern of basing economic decisions on the recent past, you need to use a decision-making framework that can see through the delusions of the crowd, and anticipate the next turn in the economy.

Good judgments are easy to make after the fact. But it is difficult to make the right decision in the heat of the moment. When it comes to gathering information for making decisions, most of us rely on sources that reflect the consensus view. Yet the consensus, like Coyote, has a dismal record of spotting turns in the road ahead.

Prevailing wisdom on the economy is delivered to you by the news media, whose ratings depend on the excitement that extreme views generate. Politicians and business leaders with their own agendas contribute to the hype. The purveyors of this collective wisdom are focused on advancing their own interests, not yours. As with most things in life, ultimately you need to watch out for yourself.

AN OBJECTIVE FRAMEWORK

As business cycle researchers, we use methods that set us apart from other economists. Our record validates our approach. We correctly forecasted major economic turning points in the United States and abroad over the past decades.[6] While there is no Holy Grail in forecasting, the discipline and objectivity of our approach have allowed us to step away from the crowd at the right time and predict turning points when most forecasters fail (see Appendix A).

Economic forecasting deserves its bad reputation in predicting recessions and recoveries. As *The Economist* noted, "In March

2001, 95% of American economists thought there would not be a recession, yet one had already started."[7] The reason for this failure is simple. Most economists forecast by extrapolating economic trends. While this methodology has its merits, forecasting turning points is not one of them.

Why does this approach fail to predict turning points? One key reason is that these forecasting models assume the recent past to be a good guide to the near future (see chart below). Most of the time this is true. But as we approach economic turning points, by definition, the pattern changes. The gap between such forecasts and reality balloons, resulting in large forecast errors.

There is a better way. By using our approach, and focusing on the right cyclical leading indicators, you can tell objectively and

A Turning Point Is Difficult to Forecast

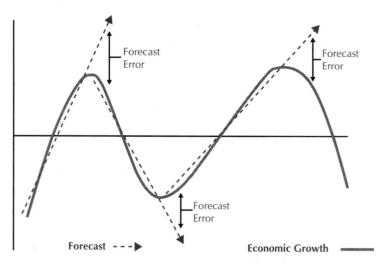

Projecting the future from past patterns can result in big errors at turning points in the economy.

unemotionally when a turn in the cycle is ahead. Unlike models that extrapolate from past trends, these cyclical indicators are specifically designed to predict future changes in the direction of the economy. They turn before the economy does. The focus is on the *timing* of a change in direction (see chart below).

At ECRI we use a cyclical approach that incorporates about one hundred objective indexes to advise governments and central banks, investment managers controlling over a trillion dollars in assets, and global companies ranging from Disney to DuPont, as well as individuals. Seeing a turning point ahead can allow a company to adjust production, inventory, pricing, and hiring. It can help an individual to decide whether it is the right time to change careers or buy a new home. It can assist an investor in making an

Leading Indexes Anticipate Turning Points

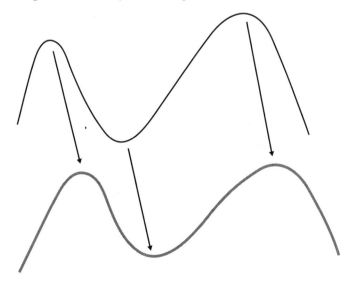

Turns in the Leading Index anticipate turns in the economy.

important shift in asset allocation. The risk of making the wrong decision is vastly reduced when the near-term direction of the economic cycle is clear. In this way, a cyclical worldview gives you or your company a critical competitive advantage.

In the following chapters, we will walk you through business cycle basics and provide a framework to help you assess and interpret current events from a cyclical perspective using publicly available information. After all, we developed the first leading indicators of recession and recovery[8] half a century ago. Moreover, you will not need to spend lots of time analyzing economic data in order to benefit from this information.

We have organized a wide range of select data into an array of leading indexes, or gauges, that will help to tell you the likelihood of a turning point taking place. Using those gauges, you can design your own "economic dashboard" to suit your particular needs.

Some businesses and individuals need an economic dashboard as sophisticated as the instrument panel in a jet cockpit. Most of us, however, need only a few warning lights—like the warning gauges in a car—and will probably need only to watch the leading indicators for inflation and economic growth. Whatever your needs, we will tell you where to get this information and how to put it to use.

People whose line of work is sensitive to economic shifts, like fund managers and corporate strategists, will want to keep a sharp eye on their dashboard, watching the indicators' every rise and fall. Most of us, however, can monitor it less closely.

Just as you do not need to know exactly how a car engine works in order to drive safely, once you set up a dashboard, you do not need to understand all the intricacies of the economy to accurately read those gauges. The economic dashboard is a simple way to help businesses and individuals avoid surprises. It acts as an early-warning system that allows you to focus on your business or career without undue worry. Doing so, you will be better positioned to make the decisions that greatly impact your company's future or your personal life.

Are you planning a leave of absence? Thinking of returning to school to get an advanced degree? Checking the leading indicators can help reassure you that the bottom will not suddenly fall out of the job market while you are away. Are you thinking of changing jobs? The gauges we discuss in the book could tell you if the effort is a good use of your energy, or one that puts your existing job at risk at precisely the wrong time. If you foresee a downturn ahead, it may make sense to focus on retaining your current job or consider breaking into a recession-proof industry.

Predicting economic turning points can even help you with respect to your financial investments. If a significant portion of your assets is invested in equities, the gauges you monitor can help you to decide whether a pullback in stock prices is merely a temporary dip, or a recession-driven bear market that calls for a shift of assets into bonds or less volatile investments. If you are a business executive trying to decide whether to expand your business or conserve your resources, our gauges can help you make the right choice at the right time.

Of course, making the right decisions about your business, job, home, or investments requires an ability to withstand peer pressure. Every day you will read or hear views from experts and pundits on where the economy is headed. But especially around turning points in the economy, these views are likely to be wrong.

A wide range of powerful constituencies have a vested interest in promoting their views about where the economy is headed.

Some will be perma-bulls who egg you on even as stock prices plunge. Others are their mirror-image—perma-bears who are so pessimistic they will miss even a history-making expansion. After the fact, these pundits may look in the rearview mirror and analyze events with considerable insight. But will they help you identify the next turning point in time to make a difference?

Since 1790, the U.S. economy has experienced forty-six business cycles. Time and again people came to believe that business cycles had been banished, only to be surprised by a new recession. No sooner had Mark Twain written about the "Gilded Age" in 1873 than a depression enveloped the economy. In the twentieth century alone, we've seen three periods hailed as "New Eras." As remarkable as it may seem, every so often we fall into the trap of believing that some new innovation, technology, or policy has paved the way for a New Era of endless prosperity, where risk and downturns are a thing of the past. It is from these heights of certainty that we tend to crash to the depths of despair, where risk seems to lurk around every corner. Neither extreme is realistic. Cycles always turn; the question is *when*. While every cycle need not exhibit a spectacular boom or bust, it is a sure bet that you will see more recessions and recoveries in the future.

Some people will remain skeptical about predicting turning points. You can choose to believe these naysayers, or join with those who use our approach to guard against unexpected swings in the economy.

Whether a mild recession or a major depression lies ahead, you can be forewarned and forearmed, protecting your interests by staying ahead of the crowd. The tools we offer will give you the confidence you need to break from prevailing wisdom as the economy approaches a turning point, and act decisively in your best interest.

A History of Cycles

Historically, upswings tend to persist for years (downswings tend to be shorter). Because of this persistence, most economists explicitly incorporate such behavior into their models of the economy. As a result, standard forecasting tools tend to work pretty well *during* upswings or downswings, but are blind to the inevitable shifts in the economy from one direction to another.

To some extent, myopia is to blame. What seems to be a time-tested trend—say, a six-year economic expansion—may only be part of a larger pattern over a longer period of time. Without a truly historical perspective, it is impossible to tell. This chapter gives you a historical overview of business cycle research and shows the fundamental ways we have parted company with all the forecasters who have failed at predicting recessions and recoveries time and again.

Early in the last century, economist Wesley Mitchell realized that in order to understand the nature of business cycles, it was necessary to collect and study the data about them. In 1920, he helped found the National Bureau of Economic Research (NBER), in large part to begin a systematic observation of the history of business cycles, both in the United States and abroad. It was a mammoth and ambitious project, and one that we continue today at ECRI.

Looking at business cycles with a broad view would provide a richer understanding of how they evolve under varying conditions. Mitchell, along with his colleague Arthur F. Burns and others at the NBER, were pioneers in uncovering the distinctive characteristics of business cycles. For example, they observed a durable sequence of economic events that occurred around cyclical turning points. Such findings laid the foundation for ECRI's methods of forecasting recessions and recoveries in free-market economies around the world.

THE BIRTH OF THE MODERN BUSINESS CYCLE

People have always known that good times come and go. The Bible says that seven years of plenty would be followed by seven lean years. In agricultural economies, changes in weather and crop yields had a direct impact on growth. Not surprisingly, one popular theory in the 1800s explained cycles in economic activity on the basis of a compelling correlation with sunspot cycles.[1]

However, it was the rise of the money-based economy that laid the groundwork for cyclical patterns in the economy. When labor could be exchanged for some form of currency, and goods could be traded for money instead of being bartered for other goods, it became possible for people to rely solely on making and spending money for their livelihoods. Governments quickly found that they could use money to facilitate the administration of duties and taxes while communities found themselves increasingly subject to a new form of swings in prosperity and depression.

The emergence of paper money resulted in even more pronounced swings. In 1716, a Scotsman named John Law convinced the French throne to set up a bank to administer national revenues and essentially issue paper money backed by gold or silver in the treasury. Shares in this new bank were sold to the public in a scheme that allowed the government to spend more than it received in taxes and other revenues. The introduction of this "paper money" greatly facilitated commerce and speculation, which soon led to a strong upswing in national prosperity. With such results, more paper money was printed.

Reaping the benefits of this financial magic, the government decided to expand the supply of paper money by issuing shares in a new venture. The now infamous Mississippi Company was granted exclusive trading rights to many potentially rich territories worldwide. In the optimistic spirit of the times, it seemed like a good bet to the general public, and the issue soon became heavily oversubscribed.

A bull market charged ahead and even more money was printed. Some speculators sensed the danger in this exuberance and began to change their paper notes back to coin and other tangible assets. The profit potential of the Mississippi Company had been based loosely on the idea that it would discover gold overseas. When gold did not turn up in Mississippi, confidence in the scheme began to crack and more people cashed in. Because the amount of gold and silver in the treasury could not equal the amount of paper notes in circulation, people quickly lost faith in paper money and began hoarding coins. The government tried in vain to deal with the falling money supply by printing even more money. However, the tide never turned and the boom collapsed under the weight of its own excesses.

Around the same time, in 1720, a venture in England known as the South Sea Scheme succumbed to a similar fate. In terms of irrational exuberance, both matched the dot-com mania and excesses of the 1990s. The eminent physicist Sir Isaac Newton, then head of the British mint, lost a small fortune in the mayhem. As he later reflected, "I can calculate the motions of the heavenly bodies, but not the madness of people." His words might have cautioned the economists of the twentieth century who aspired to develop economic forecasting models that had the simplicity and elegance of Newtonian physics.

While a money-based economy plays a key role in the modern business cycle, the rise of industrialization cemented the cyclical nature of our free markets. An industrialized economy requires a different form of organization than does the agrarian model. Financing is needed to set up industrial capacity (for example, the building of factories). Credit is extended and debts are incurred on the assumption that both sides will profit. Furthermore, industrial production requires that a chain of inventory be set up among geographically diverse suppliers. This naturally increases uncertainty in production and pricing and also builds time delays into market reactions. The waxing and waning of profits at different stages of the production cycle drive decisions about how much of a good to produce, how much to buy, and at what price. Furthermore, as firms grow in size, with relatively few employers responsible for many employees, each decision of those employers affects a lot of people at once.

Together, these factors introduced endogenous, or internal, forces that feed back into economic activity. Before the industrial sector came to dominate the economy, external forces such as weather, war, and even plague drove the economy up and down. By their very nature, these external shocks are not predictable through economic forecasting. When decisions about prices, production, employment, and financing began to dominate the economic cycle, it became more reasonable—in principle—to try to predict the turns.

This hardly stopped people from continuing to blame external shocks whenever a cyclical downturn occurred. In 1990, some blamed the U.S. recession on Iraq's invasion of Kuwait. In 2001, the terrorist attacks were similarly cited as the reason for our most recent recession. Such "attribution bias" is part of human nature. In France in the 1720s, John Law was hailed as a financial genius one month and driven out of the country by a vengeful mob the next. In the late 1990s, New Economy pioneers could do no wrong, yet many people subsequently blamed them for the bust that followed.

BRINGING ORDER TO THE DEBATE

But if external shocks do not cause downturns, why do they occur? Over the centuries a variety of theories have emerged to explain business cycles.

As noted, some traced business cycles to physical influences—such as sunspots—affecting the economy.[2] Another theory was based on the notion that the alignment of Venus influenced the weather.[3] The weather was also invoked as a determinant of physical, and thus emotional, well-being that colored attitudes toward business.[4] Others focused on the psychological stages of the credit cycle,[5] or the endless chain of optimistic and pessimistic error.[6] A third and much larger group looked at the impact of institutions or institutional change on business cycles. This included, most prominently, economist Joseph Schumpeter, who observed early in the twentieth century how innovation comes in waves to spur periods of economic expansion.[7] Still other theories focused on the impact of prospective profits on business confidence, changes in orders affecting changes in purchases, and fluctuations in consumer incomes, production, liquidity, and prices.

According to Wesley Mitchell, many of these theories had merit in explaining some particular circumstance. But they were not synthesized in a way that would explain all the different phenomena of the business cycle. The problem was far too complex. While there were historical records of business cycles that described specific economic crises that had occurred around downturns, they did not shine any light on common patterns that could be used to better understand the essential nature of the cycle.

Mitchell brought order to the debate by establishing a straightforward framework to address the problem. He felt that the only reasonable basis for properly understanding business cycles was to first collect and study the observational data. From these facts, theories could be generated to suggest relationships.

Theories that did not work in practice would be rejected. Over time, he hoped, business cycles would be understood in more detail and accuracy. Given the complexity of the business cycle and its setting, he did not expect to come up with a complete theory quickly.

But Mitchell's approach was predicated on exhaustive, long-term study. Looking at business cycles in such a systematic way began to yield dividends from the start. For the first time, a definition of modern business cycles was enunciated. According to Mitchell:

> *Business cycles are a type of fluctuation found in the aggregate economic activity of nations that organize their work mainly in business enterprises: a cycle consists of expansions occurring at about the same time in many economic activities, followed by similarly general recessions, contractions, and revivals which merge into the expansion phase of the next cycle; this sequence of changes is recurrent but not periodic; in duration business cycles vary from more than one year to ten or twelve years; they are not divisible into shorter cycles of similar character with amplitudes approximating their own.*[8]

This definition provided researchers with the first map of the territory they had set out to explore. Once the borders had been drawn, they helped guide future explorations.

By looking at the times when the cycle changed direction, NBER researchers began to discover important economic relationships. These relationships revealed consistent sequences of events around cycle turning points. For example, new orders would turn down before production did, which in turn would be followed by a rise in the duration of unemployment. While the discovery of such patterns was significant, Mitchell knew that much more observation was needed before any general theory of the business cycle could be developed.

In 1929, research met reality head-on. The speculative euphoria surrounding the first "New Era" of the twentieth century—a so-called permanent plateau of prosperity—ended suddenly with the stock market's Great Crash. The contraction that followed was deep and prolonged. Business cycle research had a practical emergency on its hands, bringing its findings to the forefront of national concerns.

In the 1930s, U.S. Treasury Secretary Henry Morgenthau Jr. asked Mitchell to determine if there were any economic variables that might point to signs of recovery. Because of his understanding of business cycles and long observation of the sequence of events around turns, Mitchell, with his associate Arthur Burns, was able to list "leading indicators of revival" that could be expected to anticipate an economic upturn. These first leading indicators were identified in their seminal 1938 paper, "Statistical Indicators of Cyclical Revivals."[9]

The outbreak of World War II shifted the nation's focus dramatically. Although the study of business cycles continued, many key figures were drawn to problems related to the war effort. Further publication of Mitchell and Burns's research had to wait until the war ended. In 1946, they published their magnum opus, *Measuring Business Cycles,* which revealed what they had determined about business cycles thus far, and set the stage for the extensive work to be done by Geoffrey Moore and the next generation of business cycle researchers.

THE RISE OF PHYSICS ENVY

In 1947, an economist named Tjalling Koopmans published a sharp rebuke of *Measuring Business Cycles* titled "Measurement Without Theory." The paper dismissed Mitchell and Burns's approach as unscientific because they relied on the extensive collection of data to observe cyclical patterns, instead of first postulating theoretical models that could be validated or rejected by the empirical data.

Koopmans spoke for a growing number of economists who wanted to apply the scientific method to economics as if it were a branch of physics or chemistry. Such desires dominate economics to this day, although "scientific" methods have repeatedly failed to predict cyclical turning points.

In the early twentieth century, it was easy to become enamored with the promise of science. From electricity to radio, a series of spectacular discoveries was transforming society, and there was a great deal of excitement and hope for what science would accomplish in the years to come. Theorists who delved into descriptive fields like economics or sociology aspired to apply the scientific method to their work in order to give it the respectability of a hard science like physics.

But what does it mean to have a scientific approach? In 1934, Sir Karl Popper, a celebrated philosopher, published *The Logic of Scientific Discovery*, which discredited a broad range of research approaches and replaced them with the idea of "falsificationism." According to Popper, in order for science to advance, only theories capable of being rejected through empirical testing, or being able to be "falsified," should be put forth. He asserted that only falsifiable theories were worthwhile because they could differentiate between valid and invalid theories. For example, one might theorize that the time it takes for a ball to fall from the top of a building is directly proportional to the square root of the height of the building. Such a theory can be easily tested, and rejected if it does not hold up. (In case you are wondering, it does.)

In contrast, Mitchell and Burns's approach to understanding economic turning points relied on descriptive observations that were not "falsifiable" like mathematical equations. Only after a great deal of observation did they attempt to come to an understanding of the dynamics that drive the business cycle. This philosophy mirrored that of another great detective, Sherlock Holmes. In "A Scandal in Bohemia," Holmes observes, "It is a capital mistake to theorize before one has data. Insensibly one begins to twist facts to suit theories, instead of theories to suit facts."[10] But to Koopmans and others swept up by Popper's philosophy, the observation-driven approach was fundamentally flawed because it was "unscientific."

This attitude was consistent with a growing trend, and in the years that followed, economists came down with a severe case of physics envy. More and more, as economists developed economic models, the ideal became the determinism of nineteenth-century classical physics.

Business cycles, however, are impossible to express in simple mathematical equations, because their complexity is rooted in human psychology. Because cycles did not lend themselves to simple scientific theories, many economists chose to ignore them. Instead they focused on linear models of the economy that could be falsified.

These simplified economic models were an attempt to mimic the past. By the 1960s, with the help of computers, economists had developed megamodels with thousands of linear equations. While they succeeded in some areas of forecasting, when it came to predicting recessions and recoveries, they failed utterly. Some economists tried to tweak their models, hoping they would work better the next time. Many others, instead of questioning whether or not their "scientific" model-building approach might be flawed, jumped to the conclusion that turning points themselves were unforecastable.

MOORE'S LONELY PATH

Geoffrey Moore disagreed. His confidence in the approach of his mentors, Mitchell and Burns, was resolute. In fact, ECRI's ability to forecast cycles today is a direct result of his single-minded focus on business cycle research.

Moore worked as a chicken farmer to pay his way through school during the Great Depression and earned a degree in agricultural economics at Rutgers University. He studied under Arthur Burns, whose enthusiasm for business cycles had a big impact on the young student. Moore wrote his doctoral dissertation at Harvard on "Harvest Cycles," a marriage of his early agricultural economics background with his new interest in business cycle research.

Moore joined the NBER research staff in the late 1930s, just as Mitchell and Burns were publishing their groundbreaking work on the leading indicators of revivals. Moore's background in agricultural economics gave him a long-term view on economic fluctuations. But at the NBER his work increasingly focused on the observation of modern business cycles.

In 1946, Moore took a year off to teach statistics at New York University. One of his students was Alan Greenspan. Greenspan was influenced by Moore, who used his mentors' landmark work, *Measuring Business Cycles,* as a primary text. "Greenspan and the other students got a taste of the NBER's rigorous approach to collecting economic data and generating statistics,"[11] noted one Greenspan biographer. Greenspan went on to do graduate work at Columbia University, partly because Mitchell and Burns taught there.

What set Moore apart from the many outstanding researchers at the NBER was his emphasis on developing practical tools to forecast business cycles. In Moore's opinion, the ability to predict cyclical turning points would be of tremendous service to policy makers and business leaders in taming the cycle's more devastating effects. By focusing on real-life issues, Moore brought business cycle research down from the ivory tower and into the everyday lives of decision makers.

This inclination made him keenly interested in the early work on leading indicators of revival. In 1950, Moore built on those findings, using data going back to the post–Civil War era to develop the first predictors of both revival and recession—that is, *leading indicators* as we know them today. Moore's selection of indicators was rooted in an understanding of the key drivers of business cycles, which he then tested against the empirical record.

The business cycle exhibits simultaneous upswings in output, employment, sales, and income, followed by similarly general downswings. It is the comovement of these variables that generates the cycle. Under certain conditions, if consumers pull back on spending, businesses respond by producing less and cutting jobs, which lowers personal incomes, hurting consumer spending further, and reinforcing the downturn. That is why during recessions all these measures of activity fall together, spreading and diffusing like wildfire. In fact, these are the key coincident indicators of the economy.

How could one predict such a shift in production? Well, if new orders fell, production would soon follow. That is, if orders were plunging, it might indicate a future downturn in production. New orders could therefore be used as a means of anticipating an imminent shift in production; in other words, it could be used as a leading indicator.

What was the significance of a shift in employment patterns? If, for example, workers were putting in more hours than usual to meet extra demand, an employer might decide to hire more people in the near future. On the other hand, if workers were idle, an employer would avoid hiring new workers and might even consider layoffs. Therefore, the average workweek should be a good leading indicator of employment. While none of these measures on its own is reliable at predicting the future direction of the economy, when properly grouped with other leading indicators, they hold a lot of valuable information.

Identifying such reliable and accurate indicators was no small accomplishment. Moore needed to be creative to develop an array of measures, or proxies, to track the drivers of business cycles, and test those indicators against the historical record. For example, corporate profits may be a leading indicator of the economy, but companies often report profits late or inaccurately. So how does one get a useful reading? Fortunately, the ratio of producer prices to the cost of labor provides a proxy for a company's profit margin and plays an important role in our cyclical forecasts. (In fact, this measure of profits correctly turned down in 1997 and kept sliding until the recession. Used alone, it would have signaled a recession too early, but in conjunction with other good indicators it was spot on.)

This process of identifying the best measures required a lot of research. Starting with the economic rationale, Moore looked at the resulting statistical indicators to see whether they passed a number of critical tests. Is it smooth enough to give clear signals? Is it extremely "noisy," jumping up and down every month? If so, it might be difficult to recognize if its path has really changed direction. Are the data promptly available? If government data are released six months after the fact, they cannot help in forecasting, even if there is a strong relationship with turns in the economy. Are the data revised a lot? If so, predictions derived from the data might be completely misleading. And, of course, does the indicator predict, or lead, peaks and troughs in the economy? If the lead is too short, an indicator's usefulness in forecasting is limited. For example, some believe that retail sales is a good harbinger of recessions and recoveries. But in fact, it moves in step with, not ahead of, the economy. So retail sales can tell you that the economy has turned only after the fact.

Such rigorous criteria found most indicators lacking. Even those that passed muster were still somewhat fallible. By its very nature, the complexity of the economy means there is neither a Holy Grail nor an exact science to cycle prediction. Because of the variety of durable feedback mechanisms, a broad spectrum of indicators is needed to represent the various drivers of the economic cycle. The risk of falsely predicting a cyclical turn can be minimized only by collecting diverse indicators in composite indexes that add up to much more than the sum of their parts.

APPLES AND ORANGES

Moore spearheaded the creation of composite indexes, a key statistical breakthrough, to resolve the dilemma of interpreting indicators that disagree at times. He needed to add together apples and oranges—radically different indicators of the economy. Most indexes are simple collections of data from similar sources—in other words, all "apples." The Dow Jones Industrial Average, for example, is an "apple" average of one kind of measure (that is, the share prices of companies). A composite index, on the other hand, is a fruit basket of measures, ranging from the hours worked by employees to the volume of new orders, from profit margins to inventory changes. This statistical innovation allowed Moore to summarize a wide range of data from an entire basket of indicators.

In coming up with a composite index, Moore created the first comprehensive gauge to warn of big shifts in the economy's direction. It cut through much of the "on the one hand/on the other hand" dispute in economic prediction. During periods of uncertainty, economic debates frequently sink into a quagmire, since for every indication of one trend there is usually evidence of a countertrend. Real estate prices are rising, so the economy must be getting stronger, one might say. But manufacturing numbers are down, so the economy must be getting weaker, says another. Composite indexes rise above such debate by objectively summarizing the data without regard to any one person's opinion.

In the early 1960s, Moore helped to develop the original composite indexes of leading, coincident, and lagging indicators of the U.S. economy,[12] which objectively summarized the data describing the durable sequence of events at turning points in the economy.

Moore wanted to better understand economic cycles and share that understanding with professional economists and laypeople alike. To that end, he gave his original set of indexes to the U.S. government. In 1968, the government adopted these composite indexes, known as the LEI, or Index of Leading Economic Indicators, as its main forecasting gauge and started releasing them in a new monthly publication called *Business Cycle Developments (BCD)*.

THE RETURN OF THE "NEW ERA"

Even decades after its end, the Great Depression remained an indelible memory for those Americans who had lived through it. At the end of World War II, many assumed that the next depression would hit with a vengeance once the economy no longer benefited from wartime expenditures. In reality, the cycle smoothed out noticeably after the war. By the late 1960s, the U.S. economy was experiencing its longest expansion on record. Many came to believe that the economy had entered a "New Era" of endless prosperity. It marked the second time in the twentieth century that such thinking had taken hold (the first was the Roaring Twenties). Many economists were eager to claim that the business cycle had been vanquished.

One of the more provocative books of 1969 was titled *Is the Business Cycle Obsolete?* Even the government seemed caught up in the euphoria. That year its publication *Business Cycle Developments*, which tracked the leading economic indicators, was renamed *Business Conditions Digest*. While the acronym (*BCD*) stayed the same, the implication was clear. The business cycle was no more.

At a conference in 1970, the eminent economist Paul Samuelson quipped that "the NBER has worked itself out of a job." After all, went the prevailing refrain, if the business cycle was a thing of the past, why bother studying it? Faced with such optimism, business cycle research seemed unnecessary. (Samuelson made his remark nine months into the recession that ended the "New Era" of the 1960s.)

In 1969, Moore took leave from the NBER to become U.S. Commissioner of Labor Statistics. When he returned to the NBER in 1973, interest in business cycles was decidedly on the wane. Unfazed, Moore continued to study the business cycles of other countries, working with Philip A. Klein to develop international composite indexes. Remarkably, they discovered that the durable sequence of leading, coincident, and lagging indicators developed for the U.S. economy were present as well in other free-market economies.

In 1974, *Scientific American* asked Moore to write an article on the forecasting methods he used to develop the Index of Leading Economic Indicators (LEI). It was a remarkable testimony to an approach that was originally criticized by the mainstream economics community as being unscientific.

Other NBER researchers made important advancements as

well. Gerhard Bry and Charlotte Boschan computerized algorithms for identifying cycle turns. Boschan also developed the first electronic macroeconomic database. Moore was quick to harness the computer for his own research. Economists had come a long way from the days when seven-foot charts of economic data were hand-drawn by a dedicated draftsman. Aided by these advancements, Moore continued to broaden his study of economic cycles.

In the late 1970s, the NBER formed a committee to date U.S. business cycles, and Moore was its senior member. He joked that before this he would "meet with myself" to determine the dates of U.S. recessions and recoveries. But as Moore neared retirement age the new leadership at the NBER shifted its focus to the "scientific approach" to economics. The NBER veered off its sixty-year path of dedicated business cycle research. For the first time in NBER history, business cycle research was placed on the back burner.

MITCHELL'S DREAM

Under the circumstances, Moore realized that in order to continue Mitchell's long-term vision, he would have to establish a new research institute. In 1979, he founded the Center for International Business Cycle Research (CIBCR) at his alma mater, Rutgers University, with the help of a small band of dedicated colleagues—including many from the NBER. Four years later, Columbia University, where Burns and Mitchell had taught, invited Moore to move CIBCR to their campus.

Over the next fifteen years at CIBCR, Moore concentrated his efforts on expanding his international economic indicators, and on developing new indicators for employment and inflation. In 1995, Moore decided to make his research institute permanently independent so that the future of business cycle research could never again be jeopardized—after all, universities are hardly immune to academic fads and fashions. He closed CIBCR and founded the Economic Cycle Research Institute—ECRI—dedicated to the tradition of business cycle research.

Unlike many research institutes, ECRI has no endowment and is not funded by any special-interest group. We cover our expenses by providing subscribers with access to our forecasts, which are based on more than one hundred cyclical indexes covering over 85 percent of world GDP.

We use this business model because it allows us to maintain our independence and preserve our objectivity. Such independence requires us to obtain funding from a diverse clientele. If we were beholden to one or a handful of institutions, our objectivity could suffer. For example, if a Wall Street investment bank or a university or the government funded our research, our views might become slanted toward the agenda of such a single backer or similar group of sponsors. Today, our broad spectrum of subscribers includes financial institutions, investment managers (both bulls and bears), Fortune 500 corporations, and policy makers around the world. ECRI publishes key information,[13] such as the Weekly Leading Index and Future Inflation Gauge without charge. For individuals who want additional information,[14] subscription reports are available that include more specialized tools, like the Leading Home Price Index.

Ironically, ECRI was founded during the third "New Era" of the twentieth century, when the business cycle was once again considered obsolete. By the end of 2001, however, it had become clear to all that the business cycle remains very much alive. And the devastating nature of the 2001 bust left many bewildered about how to go forward.

Why the Economy Rises and Falls

N ear the height of the 1990s bull market, during the longest expansion in U.S. history, Senator Daniel Patrick Moynihan, in a TV interview with Sir David Frost, reflected that the taming of the business cycle was our greatest accomplishment of the twentieth century. Considering all the medical and technological advancements that he could have mentioned, his choice may have seemed surprising to many. But he was keenly aware of the degree to which people's lives have been scarred by severe recessions, and had seen how our lives had improved as a result of milder swings in the economy. Moynihan was careful not to claim too sweeping a victory (he never said that the business cycle had been eradicated).

The recession of 2001 proved that reports of the business cycle's demise had been greatly exaggerated. Ironically, the foundation for such claims was based on a *taming* of the economic cycle that was quite real. To understand how so many came to mistakenly believe that a tamed cycle meant that cycles had been eliminated, we need to look at what caused us to have smoother cycles in the first place.

Though today's recessions are painful, they pale in comparison to those experienced by our forefathers. In 1929–33, during the Great Depression, GDP fell 35 percent and unemployment rose above 25 percent. Following World War II, recessions became much less severe. In the 2001 recession, for example, GDP fell only 0.5 percent and unemployment rose to 6.4 percent. In fact, while recessions do remain part and parcel of our free-market economy, they have been tamed considerably.

GDP and Unemployment: A Long View

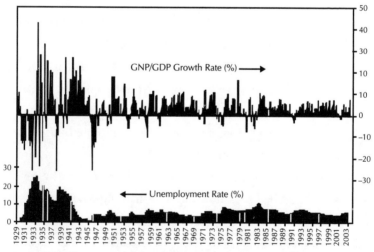

The swings in growth and unemployment have been tamed significantly since the Great Depression.

AUTOMATIC STABILIZERS

The Great Depression made an indelible mark on a generation of Americans. It showed just how severe an economic downturn could be. A quarter of the population was unemployed. Personal income was devastated. Demand disappeared, and the recession snowballed into depression. The downward momentum seemed unstoppable.

President Roosevelt's "New Deal" tried to counter the extreme downturn by introducing "automatic stabilizers" for the economy. In addition, although these were not purely cyclical in effect, Congress enacted Social Security legislation, a more progressive tax policy, and a work program to provide a temporary lift to the economy. Individual bank accounts were insured up to $100,000. In the event of job loss, legislation providing for unemployment insurance gave people a cushion to pay for basic needs, artificially introducing a base level of demand that would be otherwise impossible. Such unemployment insurance payments are considered automatic stabilizers in that if you lose your job, you automatically receive unemployment benefits. Along with helping the jobless immediately, such stabilizers also reduce the size of downturns in the business cycle itself.

SERVICE SECTOR SMOOTHING

The swings in the cycle have also been smoothed during the twentieth century by a major long-term trend in the economy: a shift from an economy dominated by the highly cyclical manufacturing sector to one led by a smoother service sector. Fifty years ago, a third of all jobs in the country were in manufacturing. Today, a mere 11 percent are employed in manufacturing, while 83 percent of Americans work in the service sector. The service sector does not experience manufacturing's large cyclical swings because it lacks inventories. Parts of the service sector remain cyclical, especially when the service provided is discretionary and can be postponed when times are tough—but the cycles are less extreme than those experienced in the manufacturing sector.

We can see the cyclical process more concretely by looking at why inventories introduce pronounced swings in demand along the production chain. In manufacturing, inventories at every stage of the process guard against shortages that could shut down production. Manufacturers, wholesalers, and retailers need enough

U.S. Coincident Services and Manufacturing Indexes

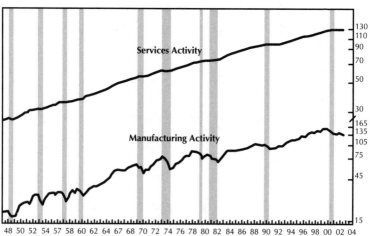

Shaded areas represent U.S. business cycle recessions. Index base year 1992=100.

Cycles in the service sector are smoother than cycles in the manufacturing sector.

raw materials or goods on hand to continue operating until the next delivery. New raw materials or goods, however, do not arrive the instant they are needed. Some stock is required to meet unexpected shifts in demand. Inventory acts as a cushion so that producers, suppliers, and retailers can continue operating without interruption.

A good illustration of how shifts in demand ripple through supply chains to produce cyclical swings can be found in an old study of the shoe, leather, and hides industries done by Ruth Mack at the National Bureau of Economic Research. Mack's 1956 study was based on early-twentieth-century data—a period during which shoes were considered a big-ticket item for many consumers, and thus a somewhat discretionary expense. Someone thinking of replacing a worn-out pair of shoes would act on that urge when they were feeling relatively prosperous. For that reason, retail shoe demand tended to be mildly cyclical. While shoes may not represent a big-ticket purchase today—at least for most of us—Mack's findings remain just as relevant to our understanding of the business cycle.

During a period of growth, the shoe manufacturer anticipates rising demand and begins to build an inventory of shoes to avoid being caught short. If the economy slows for whatever reason, some concerned consumers will react by postponing shoe purchases. Even if this results only in a *slower increase* in shoe demand—one that falls short of expectations—the shoe manufacturer will be stuck with excess shoe inventory. In addition, earlier orders to the leather producers continue to be filled, and the shoe manufacturer's inventory of leather also piles up.

Before the slowdown, the shoe manufacturer might have kept on hand a month's worth of shoe inventories to meet anticipated demand. Now, with two months' worth of inventories in place, he will not need any more leather—even should demand increase—for at least the next month. While he may not stop orders for leather completely, he is very likely to reduce new orders.

Now let us look farther down the supply line to the leather manufacturer. Mack found that slower growth in shoe sales resulted not in a slow easing of demand for leather, but in a sudden plunge. In turn, the leather producers, stuck with an even larger excess of inventories than the shoe manufacturers, turn to their suppliers of hides and cut orders still more sharply. The hides producers experience an even more precipitous drop in demand than the leather makers do. Mack's study demonstrated how the cycle becomes more pronounced the farther you get from the consumer, cascading in ever-larger cycles the closer you come to the earliest supplier in the chain.

This transmission of larger and larger cycles to suppliers earlier in the supply chain has a direct impact on prices, which are determined by both supply and demand. Slaughterhouses are not going to stop slaughtering cows because the demand for hides has plummeted. Hides, after all, are a by-product of meat production. But if the demand for hides plunges while their production does not, hides prices start to plunge. In fact, this sensitivity makes the price of hides a good leading indicator of turns in the economy. To this day, it is used as one of eighteen components in the *Journal of Commerce*–ECRI Industrial Materials Price Index, which we developed in 1986 specifically to anticipate economic turning points. Other components range from the prices of nickel, benzene, and burlap to the prices of polyester and tallow (the animal fat used to make soap).

This vicious cycle eventually turns virtuous. At some point, consumers can no longer put off the purchase of new shoes. Once demand rises slightly, the shoe manufacturer, who had previously reduced orders for leather, accelerates shoe production and needs to order additional leather. As shoe and leather orders increase, inventories are depleted and prices at every stage of the supply chain begin to climb. The largest price increases occur in hides, where demand quickly outpaces supply. Mack's study shows how the inventory cycle drives the goods-producing part of the economy, as mild fluctuations in consumer demand lead to violent demand swings at the start of the supply chain.

The shoe-leather-hides sequence that Mack studied reveals the way the manufacturing sector, driven by its inventory supply chain, magnifies booms or busts. This relationship continues to hold true today in many industries, where the production of materials used early in the supply chain cannot be shut down so easily. Much like hides, the prices of copper, silicon chips, or crude oil, to name a few, change dramatically when cyclical shifts in demand occur, because the supply of these items is determined by less flexible elements.

These strong swings in the cycle are the reason some of the world's largest manufacturing companies come to us for help in predicting turning points in demand—companies such as Toyota and DuPont, as well as leaders in the heavy machinery, mining, and transportation sectors. These firms know that they have to embrace the economic cycle and learn to anticipate its twists and turns if they want to survive and prosper.

Because services-oriented businesses have fewer inventories, their sector of the economy is less prone to the cascading cycles that dominate the manufacturing sector. Services like medicine or education are inherently less cyclical than either agriculture or manufacturing, because they cannot be stockpiled as inventories, which need to be run down when demand slackens and built up when demand rises. A barber, for example, cannot build an inventory cushion of haircuts. By their very nature, such services are produced "just in time." This is not to say that the service sector does not experience any economic cycle—it does, but on a more gentle scale.

As a result, the long-term shift toward a services-oriented economy has reduced the economy's exposure to violent inventory cycles. As the manufacturing activity that had historically been one of the primary drivers of the cycle became less dominant, so, too, did the volatility of the economy overall. This contributed to a trend toward shallower cycles in the postwar period. Nevertheless, many services, like advertising and consulting, remain highly cyclical, not because of inventories but because they still rely on discretionary expenditures that can be postponed without immediate consequences.

The Boom and
Bust of the 1990s

4

In the 1990s, even the inventory cycle began to look as if it was being tamed by various advancements in management. In the 1980s, a major concern of U.S. businesses was Japanese economic domination. Part of Japan's strong growth came from business innovations, such as strict quality control and just-in-time (JIT) inventory supply-chain management.

JIT was designed to squeeze the amount of inventory along the supply chain in order to minimize inventory-carrying costs. During the late 1990s boom, JIT supply-chain management began to play an important role in the West as well. Many companies took the Japanese innovation and coupled it with productivity-enhancing information technology (IT) investments.

The idea was simple. Computer networks had evolved to such an extent that we could use them to transmit up-to-the-minute information about demand throughout the supply chain. This approach eliminated the time lag that had amplified the volatility of inventory cycles in the past. In other words, the leather producer would learn of the shoe manufacturer's slowing demand instantly. He would immediately shoot this information to the producer of hides. By reducing the time lag of surprise, each stage of the inventory cycle would have less of a need for stockpiling inventories. Unfortunately, while this helped reduce the risk of holding inventories, producers located early in the supply chain still had to bear the brunt of any shift in demand.

Cheerleaders of the New Economy viewed this application as a technological tonic that would eliminate the inventory cycle itself. In fact, the impact IT-driven supply-chain management had on reducing cyclical volatility was overestimated. It was a costly error, one that contributed to the delusion of the New Era.

GROWING EXPERTISE

The final chapter of the New Economy story lay in growing monetary policy expertise. A decade into Alan Greenspan's tenure as chairman of the Federal Reserve, the idea that more skillful monetary policy could result in a smoother cycle was used to make the case that the business cycle itself had been repealed. Many business leaders believed that the choices we were making as a country, in terms of management and economic policy, were responsible for the smoother cycle and therefore something we could manage and control indefinitely.

One of the first major events on Greenspan's watch as Fed chairman was the 1987 stock market crash following Black Monday. In contrast to the aftermath of the crash of 1929, emergency cuts in the federal funds rate in the wake of the 1987 plunge successfully calmed the markets and the economy remained on track.

In 1989, with another potential downturn approaching, Greenspan started cutting interest rates in anticipation of a recession, a move that would mark his first attempt at generating a "soft landing." The rate cuts surprised the markets, which were worried about inflation. But they were not enough. A recession began in July 1990 (even though in its early months, many, including Greenspan, denied it was taking place). Eventually the rate cuts helped turn the economy around, and a mild recovery began in March 1991.

By early 1994, underlying inflationary pressures were rising sharply. But the market was looking the other way. Greenspan tried to generate a soft landing with a preemptive tightening of interest rates—that is, by raising rates before there was an actual rise in inflation. Seven rate hikes occurred in a one-year period; once the economy began to slow, the Fed eased interest rates, and this time the preemptive strike worked. Economists were surprised by the success of the Fed's fine-tuning; essentially the Fed had capped the rise in inflation without triggering a recession. However, the Fed's success was a mixed blessing, because it caused experts to feel that the Fed had more control over the economy than it had.

In 1997, a sharp devaluation of Thailand's currency precipitated what became known as the Asian Crisis. Financial experts feared global contagion from the "Asian flu." But the new believers of the "end of the business cycle" argued that fundamental changes in supply-chain management, globalization, and enhanced monetary policy expertise would combine to protect the U.S. economy from such shocks. To them, the Asian Crisis was the acid test. When the U.S. economy continued to grow despite the crisis, the belief that the business cycle had been conquered was taken as fact, and the pitch of "New Era" cheerleading rose to new highs.

The Asian Crisis did, however, lead to a collapse in worldwide oil demand. Russia, which was just beginning its first market-driven business cycle, felt this plunge keenly since its economy relied heavily on revenues from oil exports to Asia. The oil price collapse reduced Russia's revenues to such an extent that it threatened to default on its international loans. Many assumed that Russia was too big and important to be allowed to fail. The International Monetary Fund (IMF) called Russia's bluff by refusing to bail it out. The resulting Russian default rocked world financial markets. It triggered the collapse of the giant hedge fund Long Term Capital Management (LTCM), an event that threatened a meltdown in the global financial system.

President Clinton called it the worst financial crisis in fifty years. Greenspan swung into action. Three Fed rate cuts later, there was a rebound in confidence in the economy and in the markets. Once again, the Fed had saved the day.

THE DELUSION OF THE NEW ECONOMY

By the late 1990s, it seemed as though we had entered an age of endless prosperity characterized by growth without inflation. The economic slowdown of 1994–95 helped keep inflation low.

Later, the Asian Crisis, a Japanese recession, and the emergence of China as a major supplier of traded goods continued to put downward pressure on inflation, gutting the ability of U.S. business to raise prices. But firms still had to contend with rising labor costs. To avoid profits being squeezed out of existence, productivity needed to be boosted.

The IT sector, with its promise of rising productivity growth and everlasting prosperity, was ready to meet this need. Wall Street was eager to help finance and exploit the stampede of demand for capital investment in technology. Industry analysts did their part to reinforce these views. The resulting boom in IT spending was fueled by soaring stock prices, which were justified, in turn, by the premise that we had entered an age of limitless growth: The business cycle was dead. As a result, stocks were deemed less risky, justifying still-higher valuations.

CYCLES OF RISK

The underestimation of risk is itself cyclical. During longer expansions, like the one we experienced in the 1990s, optimism spreads as memories of past recessions fade. With optimistic assumptions bolstered by a history of continued growth, people become increasingly dismissive of risk. This causes the economy to behave in a boomlike fashion, further reinforcing such wishful thinking.

Wall Street was hardly alone in its love of higher stock prices, and the media played along. As stocks like Qualcomm rocketed twentyfold in a year, investors ranging from CEOs to mail room clerks began dreaming of untold riches and early retirement. With ready access to bull market capital, companies made giant investments in capacity, certain that the economy would continue to grow. For individuals, higher salaries, better job opportunities, and confidence in the stock market led to the false impression of financial security. These expectations about the future of the stock market were embodied in the 1999 best-seller *Dow 36,000,*[1] which declared that stock valuations at the time were far below where they should be (the Dow had recently broken 10,000). This message was just what people wanted to hear. "Buy-on-dips" seemed like a rational investment strategy, especially if a recession, and thus a major bear market, was never going to occur. Reinforcing that belief, the stock markets soared.

International events also appeared to support the view that risk was in retreat. The Cold War was over and capitalism had triumphed. As globalization advanced and nations fell in line behind the American model, it seemed that economic threats from abroad would continue to recede. Peace was widespread. And when war did occur, it seemed limited and far away. Technology kept American casualties low and made the conflicts seem relatively risk-free.

In a world where economic and physical security was taken for granted, it was easy to believe the good times would continue. In retrospect, the rising popularity of extreme sports during this period might be seen as an attempt to artificially inject risk into our lives. In an age void of risk, danger became fun.

The irrational exuberance of the late nineties bears a striking resemblance to the Roaring Twenties. In the late 1920s, the promise of new technologies and the exhilaration of a stock market bubble convinced both experts and ordinary people that the business cycle was a thing of the past. In 1929, the influential Yale University economist Irving Fisher commented that the economy had attained a permanent "plateau of prosperity." A few months later, the markets crashed.

Clearly, the investment boom helped boost economic growth. At the same time, falling import prices caused by global over-capacity from recessions abroad helped keep a lid on inflation. To believers of the "New Economy," however, it was the rise in productivity growth *alone* that enabled firms to maintain prof-itability without raising prices. As such, the story went, it was possible to permanently raise the economy's growth rate without triggering an increase in inflationary pressures.

In line with this view, New Economy cheerleaders also believed that the Fed would have less need to raise rates to head off infla-tion. The analysts' basic pitch was simple. With productivity rising sharply, companies could produce goods more cheaply and the economy could grow faster without igniting inflation. This, coupled with the elimination of inventory cycles due to IT-powered supply-chain management, and the Fed's newfound ability to manage any unexpected crises, suggested that the economy would be far less cyclical than before.

To the cheerleaders, this effectively meant that the economy would have a higher average or trend rate of growth, with smaller fluctuations in the cycle. Economic growth was now less likely to fall below zero—in other words, into recession territory. The risk of recession had been so reduced that the business cycle—the bane of the capitalist system—had finally been eradicated. This was the core of the delusion that marked the New Era of the 1990s.

BEHIND THE VEIL

Such thinking was, of course, a fantasy. Behind the veil lay a harsher reality. The fallacy of the New Economy proponents was in assuming that the reduction in business cycle volatility was caused by controllable factors, as well as by permanent changes to the economy. In fact, the remarkable period of strong noninflationary growth owed much to a run of good luck, particularly in the international arena.

It is not commonly known, even among economists, that the 1990s was a period dominated by asynchronous global recessions. This means that key economies took turns going into recession. As we will see, the timing of those offsetting recessions proved fortunate for the U.S. economy.

Why were so few aware of this pattern? One reason is that many observers, including those in countries like Japan, had come to use the word "recession" to mean something quite different from what it meant in the United States. Following World War II, countries like Japan and Germany saw long periods of virtually uninterrupted expansions, which made it difficult for them to see the relevance of classical business cycle contractions as defined by below-zero growth. Instead, they began to focus on alternating periods of above- and below-trend growth as the primary way to monitor cyclical fluctuations in their economies (if the average growth rate is 4 percent, growth at only 2 percent is below trend). To further muddle matters, these periods of below-trend growth began to be called recessions.

Given this blurring of terms, it is not surprising that Japan is widely viewed to have experienced a decade-long recession during the 1990s, even though Japanese GDP grew at a 3 percent annual rate from late 1993 to early 1997, and almost as fast in 1999 and 2000. Labeled recessions in Japan because they were marked by below-trend growth, these periods remain business cycle expansions according to the classical definition. Yet, because Japan's 1980s stock market—like the U.S. market in the late 1990s—had been driven up on the premise of permanently strong growth, even below-trend growth was disappointing. This disappointment resulted in a long bear market in stocks that further confused perceptions about the state of the Japanese economic cycle.

Geoffrey Moore long realized the benefits of accurately comparing business cycles across countries. Under Moore's guidance, ECRI painstakingly established authoritative business cycle dates for all major economies comparable to the U.S. business cycle chronology (see Appendix B). Doing so provided us with unique insights into the nature and timing of international cycles. In the 1990s, this analysis revealed the hidden role that asynchronous global recessions played in supporting growth without inflation in the United States.

The international business cycle chronology shows that the 1990s began with an "English-speaking recession," involving the United States, the United Kingdom, Canada, Australia, and New Zealand. Timing-wise, just as those economies began to recover, Japan and continental Europe went into recession.

Not until 1994 did all the major economies begin expanding in sync. The resulting boost in worldwide demand triggered an increase in U.S. import prices. ECRI's Future Inflation Gauge, or FIG, started rising at this time, indicating that underlying inflationary pressures were increasing. The Fed, in full agreement with this view, raised interest rates aggressively in 1994 to slow the economy and head off rising inflation. This move caught many off guard; few were aware that inflationary pressures were being driven by the synchronous global expansion. The Fed's rate hikes particularly surprised the bond market; 1994 was the worst year of its six-decade history, and as a result, several well-known investment funds suffered severe losses from which they never recovered. Orange County, California, actually went bankrupt. Nevertheless, the preemptive strike worked and the Future Inflation Gauge fell. A global slowdown resulted, curbing inflation as intended and creating the so-called "soft landing" of 1994–95, where the economy cooled but avoided recession.

In early 1997, a poorly timed tax hike pitched Japan into a deep business cycle recession. Later that year, the Asian Crisis

Future Inflation Gauge and Fed Funds Rate, 1988–1998

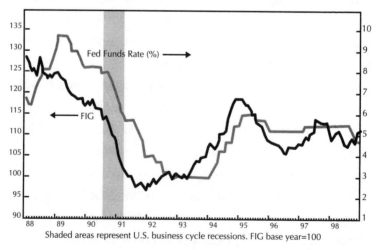

Shaded areas represent U.S. business cycle recessions. FIG base year=100

As the Future Inflation Gauge rose and fell from 1988 to 1998, the Federal Funds Rate—the rate set by Greenspan and the Federal Reserve Board—followed.

unfolded, triggering a series of currency devaluations and the first genuine business cycle recession that the Asian "tigers" had seen in decades. The resulting global glut of goods caused U.S. import prices to fall for four straight years, from 1995 to 1999. It was this, more than anything else, that was the key to the noninflationary growth experienced by the United States in the second half of the 1990s, as a New York Fed study[2] later indicated. Throughout that period, ECRI's Future Inflation Gauge correctly predicted no danger of inflation, while ECRI's separate leading indexes of growth remained strong. In other words, economists and the media did not need to invoke a "new paradigm" to explain and forecast growth without inflation.

THE ATTRIBUTION BIAS

Nonetheless, many economists attributed the inflation-free growth to productivity increases and technology. They talked about the IT-enhanced "productivity miracle" and chose to ignore the fortuitous timing of global developments that were completely beyond business leaders' and policy makers' control. This is an example of what psychologists call "attribution bias," the tendency people have to take credit for good outcomes while blaming other people or circumstances for bad outcomes.

The New Economy was an example of attribution bias on a national scale. Because we had chosen to use technology to manage inventories and raise productivity, it supposedly produced a "New Era" of inflation-free growth, a New Era that need never end. The same was true of our monetary policy actions. But attributing inflation-free growth to these factors held more risk than most imagined.

In the area of monetary policy, for instance, there was growing faith among investors in the ability of the Federal Reserve to keep recessions at bay. When the Long Term Capital Management (LTCM) crisis was contained as a result of a Fed-arranged bailout backed up by three emergency rate cuts, it inspired the further belief that the Fed could manage external shocks.

The faith in the Fed's ability to avert crises came to be known as the "Greenspan put," an analogy to a "put option" that protects the holder of the option from a market decline. In conjunction with Wall Street's new justifications for higher stock valuations, the Greenspan put reinforced the "buy-on-dips" stock investing philosophy, since every dip was supposed to be limited and thus an opportunity to buy valuable stocks more cheaply.

As the economy boomed, joblessness fell, incomes rose, and stock prices climbed. Consumers went on a buying binge, borrowing more than ever before and driving the savings rate down dramatically. After all, there was no reason to save for a rainy day if rain had been removed from the forecast.

Or had it? In 1998, on the international front, several key Asian economies began to export their way out of recession. In 1999, even the Japanese economy began to expand—though few believed it. Japan had supposedly been mired in recession for so long that no one anticipated a recovery.

MORE BIASES

This kind of thinking exemplifies another psychological term: "persistence bias," the tendency to extrapolate past performance into the future. As we have already discussed, once people get used to a pattern of events, they expect that pattern to persist, whether it is a straight road as in a Wile E. Coyote cartoon, an "endless" expansion in the United States, or a "hopeless" recession in Japan.

Objective tools allow for a clearer assessment. ECRI's Japanese Long Leading Index, for example, which consistently "turns" ahead of turns in the economy, rose sharply in 1999, correctly predicting the brief Japanese recovery. From an international perspective, this was no mere blip but rather an event with significant ramifications; Japan's recovery would radically shift the role import prices had played in keeping U.S. domestic inflation in check. According to ECRI's Future Inflation Gauge, the stage was being set for a global rise in underlying inflationary pressures.

And that is how it played out. In 1999–2000, a world that had completely written off Japan got blindsided by a synchronous global expansion for only the second time in a decade. As a result, the overcapacity abroad that had been keeping U.S. inflation pressures low began to disappear, boosting U.S. import prices. In sharp contrast to the previous four years, existing domestic inflation pressures were now being reinforced, rather than neutralized, by the prices of imports and industrial commodities.

The idea of noninflationary growth (credited to the productivity miracle) was now under attack. Would the Fed continue to support the tenets of the New Era cheerleaders? Its actions spoke louder than words. Without explicitly saying so, the Fed effectively abandoned the "new paradigm" of inflation-free growth by beginning a series of aggressive interest rate hikes to rein in underlying inflationary pressures, much as it had in 1994. Unfortunately, unlike 1994, this preemptive strike failed to subdue inflation while skirting recession.

At first New Economy devotees reasoned that the Fed's rate hikes were designed to "take back" the three rate cuts made in the wake of the LTCM fiasco. But the FIG, which is designed to lead inflation cycles, revealed that underlying inflationary pressures were rising strongly. The Fed raised rates to pre-LTCM levels and then kept going. Nor was the Fed alone in its actions. Every major central bank around the world, including the Bank of Japan, followed suit.

These concerted global interest rate hikes planted the seeds of a global slowdown intended to cool inflation pressures. The slowdown arrived on schedule in the second half of 2000. The Organization of Petroleum Exporting Countries (OPEC), along with the rest of the world, had been surprised by the rise in global energy needs resulting from synchronized growth. With demand suddenly outstripping supply, oil prices began to spike just when the world's economies began to slow. Unfortunately, those higher oil prices acted like a tax on already slowing economies.

U.S. growth decelerated sharply in the context of this global downturn. By late 2000, it had entered a window of vulnerability, where a mere push could tip the economy into recession. That push came from an unexpected source.

THE "I" OF IT

Throughout the 1995 slowdown and even the 1990–91 recession, the information technology, or IT, sector continued to grow. Many considered this proof positive that the IT sector was immune to recessions. But other explanations are more convincing.

During earlier downturns, IT had accounted for a relatively small proportion of U.S. capital spending and could buck the trend in the overall economy. But by the year 2000, IT spending accounted for almost *half* of all capital investment—meaning that, regardless of past experience, IT spending could no longer be immune to economy-wide downturns in capital investment.

With the end of the business cycle a growing article of faith, the perceived risk of overbuilding capacity was greatly diminished. Coupled with the availability of cheap capital from the stock market and the banks, capital investment in IT was deemed a low-risk proposition.

The final boost to the "bubble economy" was provided by the Y2K scare. On the verge of the year 2000, the fear of system failures prompted many companies to make major IT-related investments. The Federal Reserve's rapid infusion of cash into the economy in the weeks preceding the New Year fueled a dizzying rise in IT stock prices. When Y2K passed without incident, the perception of general risk declined even further.

Meanwhile, by mid-2000, ECRI's international long leading indexes were forecasting a synchronized global slowdown that was sure to cause a significant drop in corporate profits. Unlike the early-1990s' "English-speaking recession," which affected only some regions of the world, this time there would be no place for companies to hide. For businesses, lower profits meant that capital expenditures would need to be slashed. Because nearly half of all capital expenditures now went to IT, this sector would not escape unscathed.

But the new IT-powered economy had banked on exponential growth projections to justify its high equity valuations. With the global slowdown, suppliers to IT firms—like the suppliers in the shoe-leather-hides sequence—were suddenly left with huge inventories and massive overcapacity. This large gap between expectations and reality triggered a collapse in IT-sector growth. Ironically, it was because the IT sector lacked the "I" of IT—the vital *information* that a cyclical downturn was imminent—that it fell so hard.

The nosedive in IT growth, coupled with the ongoing slow-down induced by interest rate hikes and the oil price spike, was the final blow to the economy. For the first time in decades, a business-led capital spending bust had triggered a recession. The sector that was supposed to reduce the volatility of the business cycle ended up intensifying it. As one former official of the New York Federal Reserve observed, "How ironic that the producers of the equipment that was supposed to eliminate the inventory cycle were themselves its foremost victims."[3]

Looking back, it is easy to say that it was all bound to end. But a quick glance at newspaper headlines from the height of the boom demonstrates how widely the belief in a New Era had been embraced. In November 1998, *BusinessWeek* pronounced, "The Only Thing We Have to Fear Is Fearful Investors." In January 1999, *The New York Times* summarized the views of the venerable American Economic Association: "Economists Reject Notion of Stock Market 'Bubble.'" And in early 2000, a *U.S. News & World Report* cover read, "Boom Times: Why There's No End in Sight." Business leaders, Wall Street analysts, policy makers, and media pundits were overwhelmingly supportive of an unrealistic outlook. This made it tough to break away from that consensus and take a contrary view.

THE BUSINESS CYCLE RESURFACES

What valuable information did our cyclical worldview offer as the recession approached? Following our Future Inflation Gauge's strong rise in 1999, it began to plunge in April 2000, indicating that inflationary pressures were turning down. Additionally, that summer there was a pervasive downturn in all twelve of our leading indexes of various aspects of U.S. economic growth. By September 2000, they had fallen to their worst readings in a decade, forcing us at ECRI to warn of the danger of a recession.

Our leading indexes continued to worsen. Four months later, the Fed switched course and started cutting interest rates

Future Inflation Gauge and Fed Funds Rate, 1988–2001

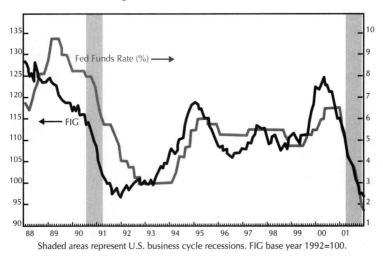

Shaded areas represent U.S. business cycle recessions. FIG base year 1992=100.

Approaching the 2001 recession, the Future Inflation Gauge correctly anticipated the rise and fall of the Fed Funds Rate.

aggressively. Since the Fed had successfully averted recessions before, many assumed it would work again. We hoped so too. But our indicators kept falling. Our final alarm went off in March 2001 when growth in our leading employment index plummeted to a nineteen-year low, alongside continuing weakness in all our other leading indexes. We knew that once people began to lose jobs in large numbers, the reality of recession would begin to hit home.

Though it was not widely recognized until much later, March 2001 marked the beginning of the first recession in the United States in ten years, and along with it, the reappearance of the business cycle.

Perceptions of risk shifted sharply when the reality of recession began to sink in. Then came September 11, 2001. The terrorist attacks altered our sense of vulnerability to external threats,

Weekly Leading Index, 1988–2001

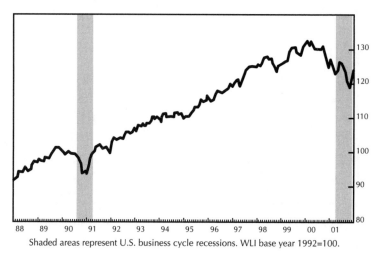

Shaded areas represent U.S. business cycle recessions. WLI base year 1992=100.

As you can see, the drop in the Weekly Leading Index anticipated the 2001 recession.

both physical and economic. The world suddenly seemed an uncertain and dangerous place.

But even before September 11, the economy had plunged into a recession and a bear market was under way. Layoffs and a falling stock market had left us feeling less secure about employment, finances, and the future in general. Soon after, the implosion of Enron, one of the poster children of the New Economy, set off a wave of corporate scandals, undercutting our faith in the leaders of big business. As in previous New Eras, the euphoria of the boom had increased the payoff for spectacular performance, causing investors to overlook signs of corporate greed and fraud. When performance began to fall short of inflated expectations, company after company resorted to increasingly creative accounting to keep the fantasy alive. WorldCom, Tyco, Arthur Andersen, and Enron were just the tip of the iceberg. The recession-driven bear market mercilessly exposed those myths and many others.

By November 2001, thanks to a ton of monetary and fiscal stimuli, which supported a rising real estate market and robust consumer spending, the recession had ended. But almost no one realized it. One key reason is the persistence of perceptions, this time blinding people to an economic upturn. Another reason was confusion between cyclical and structural economic shifts, manifested in this recovery by a loss of jobs, particularly in the manufacturing sector. Accelerated by a global recession, this structural change was the unintended consequence of three long-term trends: the two-decade fight against inflation by the Fed and other central banks; the increasing impact of productivity-enhancing technologies; and the growing integration of China into the global economy.

Recessions kill inflation. But when inflation is already low, a recession that creates global overcapacity produces deflationary pressures in tradable-goods prices. Because companies making those goods lack pricing power, they must cut costs in order to survive. Rather than adding to payrolls, companies cut costs. They did so both by increasing productivity and by outsourcing production to cheaper foreign factories. The combination resulted in a huge loss of U.S. manufacturing jobs, jobs that are unlikely to be replaced, even though the economy is in a cyclical recovery. Without a cyclical worldview, it is difficult to understand the reality of this recovery and the unique opportunities and risks it holds.

Nonetheless, Senator Moynihan, quoted early in the chapter, was correct in saying that the business cycle had been *tamed*. That was an important accomplishment, because it alleviated the broad suffering caused by deep depressions, allowing for steadier growth and longer periods of prosperity. But it is wishful thinking to extrapolate from this positive development and suggest that recessions have been eradicated. In fact, that very mentality guarantees the resurgence of the cycle. Once businesses, policy makers, and individuals begin to act on the assumption that recessions are unlikely, they make decisions that are inherently more risky. The true risk is made obvious only by the recession's unequivocal arrival—much too late for those who overextended themselves.

It is understandably difficult to escape from illusions like the New Era when they are so widely and confidently reinforced. Unfortunately, it is all but certain that such illusions will occur again. Someday we will experience another time when a downturn in the economy appears impossible. And each bust will inevitably be followed by the resurrection of perceived risk, where danger seems to lurk around every corner. It takes time for confidence in the economy to reemerge. Gradually, the pain of the downturn recedes from collective memory and the focus turns to the next expansion. But if you wait for popular opinion to inform you of an upturn, you'll be too late. For example, concerns about a double-dip recession did not begin to fade until the summer of 2003, almost two years into the recovery. We know of an armchair economist who was so pessimistic in late 2001 that he sold his home, believing that ECRI's call for a recovery was crazy. He thought prices would drop and that he could soon buy another home at a much lower price. Unfortunately for him, home prices kept climbing and he is still renting.

Such behavior should be a thing of the past. With the tools that we present in this book, both businesses—large and small—and individuals will be able to "see" the economic road ahead, make decisions that will give them an edge over the competition, and allow them to break out of the herd mentality that has waylaid so many. In Part Two, we discuss the key advancements that enable us to see through the fog. In Part Three, we show you how to use a cyclical worldview to guide your business and personal decisions.

It is impossible to remove the cycle from a free-market economy. But by understanding the nature of business cycles and employing a cyclical view in your decision making, you can protect yourself from falling prey to "prevailing wisdom" the next time the cycle turns.

PART TWO

Leading
Indicators 101

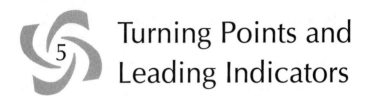

Turning Points and Leading Indicators

THE DEFINITION OF THE BUSINESS CYCLE

Each recession is unique, triggered by a different set of factors. This leads to wide latitude in assessing blame for a contraction, even among experts. For example, even though the 2001 recession began in March, some will forever link it to the terrorist attacks of September 11 or the corporate scandals that followed. Other recessions have been blamed on oil shocks, on the crisis in the Middle East, and on Federal Reserve interest rate hikes. While external shocks like these can help precipitate a recession, they are seldom the cause.

Similarly, each recovery has unique characteristics. In the recovery that followed the 2001 recession, the job market remained very weak while growth was rebounding. One key difference between this and other recoveries was the dramatically accelerated loss of manufacturing jobs. But as we have suggested before, there are patterns common to all recessions and recoveries that can be used to understand and forecast the timing of turns in the cycle. Decades of observation have shown us that during a typical recession, companies fire employees, incomes fall, spending goes down, and output declines. By examining the historical record, we know that, during recessions, these four factors—employment, income, output, and sales—tend to decline together.

This comovement of all four factors is key. On occasion, a temporary dip in one or more of these variables may occur. But only during a recession—or cyclical downturn—will all four measures decline together. (During some mild recessions, income *growth* has slowed, though incomes did not drop.)

We also know that during a cyclical downturn, declines in employment, income, sales, and output feed on one another, snowballing into an avalanche. When people lose jobs, incomes fall. As a result, they buy less, which means companies produce less and therefore need fewer employees. Additional layoffs result, leading to a further drop in income, a further drop in sales, and a further decline in output.

When people lose jobs in one or more industries, they reduce their spending in many different areas. Because of this, the downturn spreads from industry to industry, often like wildfire, until it engulfs most of the economy. For similar reasons, recessions can spread from region to region.

At cyclical upturns, the vicious cycle turns virtuous and the mirror image of those events occurs. Sales, output, income, and

A Virtuous Cycle

Feedback loop that occurs during a recovery, showing the linkage among the four key coincident indicators of the economy.

employment all increase in unison. With people buying more, industries produce more, which typically requires them to hire more people, causing incomes to rise. The effects spread from industry to industry and region to region, until the expansion encompasses most of the economy.

These observations form the basis of the classic definition of business cycles in market economies established by Wesley Mitchell in 1927. Here are the key points:

- Business cycles are fluctuations in aggregate economic activity.
- A cycle consists of simultaneous expansions in many economic activities, followed by similarly general recessions.

- This sequence of changes is recurrent but not periodic; cycles can last from one year to ten or twelve years.
- They are not divisible into shorter cycles of similar magnitude and character.

This definition provides clarity when it comes to determining if a recession has begun, unlike the popular misleading "two down quarters of GDP" rule of thumb, according to which, if GDP falls for two straight quarters, we have met the "technical" definition of a recession. GDP is just a measure of an economy's output. But if employment, income, and sales do not fall at the same time, the temporary period of negative-output growth will not catch on and spread, and no recession will occur. That is why such simplistic "rules" can lead to greater risk for decision makers.

For example, in July 2002, when the data showed GDP falling only during the third quarter of 2001, U.S. Treasury Secretary Paul O'Neill asserted that the economy had not been in a recession. Later that month, when the revised data finally revealed that GDP had been negative in each of the first three quarters of 2001, the reality of recession dawned on many doubters, sixteen long months after it had started. Similarly, it was not until June 1998, when the two-down-quarters-of-GDP "rule" had been satisfied, that many finally accepted that Japan was in recession, fifteen months after it began.

In contrast to such simplistic "rules," the classical definition of business cycles is a sophisticated description of what occurs at cyclical upturns and downturns and is used to officially date business cycles in the United States. Understanding it is vital. This knowledge will serve you well the next time confusion reigns about whether a recession has begun or if a recovery is for real.

MORE THAN JUST SEMANTICS

An additional source of confusion in the debate about recessions and recoveries has to do with clarity of terms. It is important to understand exactly what we mean when we talk about various cycles.

In 1999, Japan's economy began to expand after a lengthy decline. Yet, because many in Japan defined recessions not by the classical definition but as a time when growth falls below its average trend rate, few believed a recovery was actually taking place. In other words, what many viewed as a continuing recession was actually a period of slower-than-average growth. Technically, these fluctuations in growth relative to trend are known as growth cycles.

During a classical business cycle recession, the economy actually shrinks or grows at a below-zero rate. A growth cycle recession, on the other hand, is defined as a period of below-trend growth. Periods of below-*trend* growth do not necessarily imply that a business cycle recession is imminent. In fact, a period of below-trend growth that does not devolve into negative growth is sometimes called a slowdown or "soft landing."

From the early 1970s to the early 1990s, growth cycles were a significant part of our international research. Many of the economies examined were experiencing long periods of expansion without classical recessions. In the two decades following World War II, Germany kept growing without a recession. Japan experienced only one recession between 1954 and 1992. Nonetheless, those economies did experience cycles in terms of their *pace* of growth. Sometimes they grew faster than the average trend, sometimes slower. Accordingly, it became useful to monitor alternating periods of above- and below-trend growth—that is, the growth cycle—in the search for similarities among different market-oriented economies.

But attempting to forecast economic turning points using the growth cycle framework was problematic, as it requires knowing the actual trend of growth at any given point in time. Historically, you can look back and calculate the trend growth rate, but you cannot know the present trend because it is very likely to be shifting under your feet.

Nevertheless, the growth cycle concept has helped us develop our understanding of economic fluctuations. In the early 1980s, groups like the Organization for Economic Cooperation and Development (OECD) embraced growth cycles and continue to use them today. Decision makers, on the other hand, cannot make choices in hindsight and have a compelling need to know what is happening now. That is why, for forecasting purposes, we focus on something different—the growth *rate* cycle—in addition to the classical business cycle.

The business cycle is made up of expansions and contractions in the overall economy. A peak in the business cycle is the point where the economy stops expanding and starts contracting—in the facing chart, this corresponds to point A. A trough in the business cycle occurs when the economy stops contracting and starts expanding (point B). Points A and B are the cyclical high and low points, respectively, of the line that represents economic activity. They are the *turning points* in the *business cycle.*

The *growth rate cycle,* on the other hand, is made up of periods of rising and falling economic growth. The growth rate cycle may

Business Cycle and Growth Rate Cycle

Adapted from Anas. J. and Ferrara. L. (2002). "Detecting cyclical turning points: The ABCD approach and two probabilistic indicators." Paper presented at the 26th CIRET Conference in Taipei, October 2002, submitted to the *Journal of Business Cycles Measurement and Analysis.*

A business cycle recession is a decline in the level *of economic activity, from point A to B. A growth rate cycle downturn is a decline in the growth rate of economic activity, from point C to D. Notice that the peak and the trough of the growth rate cycle precede the peak and the trough of the business cycle.*

---

be in a downturn, even though the economy is still expanding (albeit more slowly). Growth rate cycles are sustained periods of simultaneous upward or downward movement in the *growth rates* of output, employment, income, and sales. Suppose you *know* that the current trend rate of growth is 3 percent. (And remember, you'll know the current trend only well after the fact.) If the economy's growth rate peaks at 5 percent and heads down, that is a *growth rate cycle* downturn. If it slips below 3 percent, it becomes a *growth cycle* recession. If the economy's growth bottoms out at 1 percent and starts heading higher, we call it a *growth rate cycle* upturn, but not until it crosses above 3 percent do we refer to it as a *growth cycle* expansion. Remember that at no point in this scenario would the economy be in a classical business cycle recession, or a contraction.

In other words, it is not enough to look at the business cycle to gauge where the economy is going. But when you combine the classical business cycle with the growth rate cycle, you have a powerful framework for real-time monitoring of the economy.

WARNING!

Readers may encounter the term "growth cycle," because it is commonly used. It can be a source of considerable confusion.

The growth cycle is not the same as the growth rate cycle. The *growth rate cycle* tracks upswings and downswings in the rate of growth of the economy, and is a very useful measurement when used in conjunction with the business cycle. *Growth cycle* analysis, however, requires that you know the growth trend at the time, since growth cycles are defined as periods of above- and below-*trend* growth. However, the trend can only be determined in hindsight. After having used the growth cycle for twenty years ourselves, we have come to realize its shortcomings. It is great for describing and analyzing historical events, but it can be misleading as a tool to help predict future turning points.

DURABLE SEQUENCES

Certain indicators, like production or sales, turn in step with the economy. Because these indicators always coincide with the economy, we can use them to track the business cycle's progress, and call them "coincident" indicators. Another group of indicators, like mortgage applications and profit margins, consistently turn *before* the economy does. We call them "leading" indicators. A separate group of indicators turn *after* the economy turns. We call those "lagging" indicators. This durable sequence is seen around cyclical turns in every market economy.

Since output, employment, income, and sales all turn up or down more or less together around the time when a cyclical turn occurs, they are considered coincident indicators. To assess the current state of the business cycle, we watch those measures closely. As we have explained, a sustained shift in these four indicators reveals that the business cycle itself is turning.

The key to making better economic decisions, however, is to know whether those coincident indicators are going to turn together in the near future. For the sake of prediction, we monitor the events that typically happen *before* cyclical turns—the shifts in the leading indicators. As discussed in the last chapter, a good indicator of an imminent shift in production might be a change in new orders, and an indicator of future employment might be the average number of hours worked. Leading indicators turn up or down around turning points, much as coincident indicators do; they simply turn earlier.

And finally, because they follow a cyclical turn in the economy, lagging indicators can provide important confirmation of what has already transpired in the business cycle.

The process of determining accurate leading, coincident, and lagging indicators is rigorous and painstaking. It is based on a theoretical understanding of the key drivers of the business cycle, followed by a great deal of empirical observation and extensive

Leading, Coincident, and Lagging Indexes

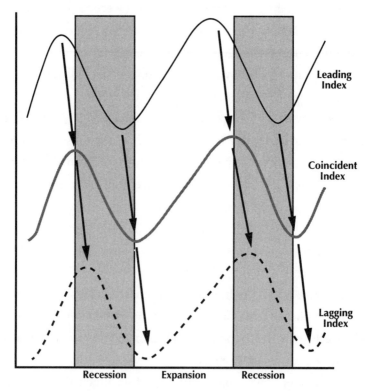

The Leading Index "turns" before the economy turns. The Coincident Index turns in step with the economy. The Lagging Index follows the economy.

real-world testing. First, the events around a cyclical turn are observed and understood in terms of their contribution to the evolution of the business cycle. In that way we learned what the drivers of the cycle were.

The durable sequences linking leading, coincident, and lagging indicators together help us to monitor the economy objectively. Without such a framework, the cross-currents in the deluge of data would obscure the economy's direction. Durable sequences capture the consistent pattern at economic turning points by filtering out the noise and distortions of subjective perspective, allowing us to make sense of the patterns that remain.

This is important for a simple reason. When we get caught up in the moment, it is only natural to assume that "this time it's different." Many find it easy to believe that dramatic events, due to their unique nature, trigger economic developments that leading indicators cannot predict. In other words, those people assume that leading indicators will fail because they cannot account for fundamentally unpredictable events such as war, financial scandals, or policy shifts. No one could have foreseen the September 11 terrorist attacks or the corporate scandals of 2001, goes the argument, so no forecasting system could have anticipated the 2001 recession. But, of course, the recession actually started six months before the attack, as we at ECRI predicted.

Another common misconception is that some unique development has so dramatically altered the economic landscape that indicators that have worked in the past have been rendered obsolete. During the 1990s, for example, information technology advances were considered to be just such a change, and were used to rationalize the notion that the New Economy did not obey the old rules.

Structural changes can alter the size of the cycle and even shift the timing of the turning point a little. But in reality, the unique events in a particular business cycle do not eliminate the durable sequence that surrounds every recession. While such events can never be included explicitly in the progressions that are monitored, they are in fact implicitly picked up by some measures, like market prices and confidence surveys. The sequences work regardless of the drama or confusion of any particular moment. They also work just as well in "normal" recessions and recoveries as they do in wilder boom-bust cycles.

As we have said before, there is no Holy Grail of forecasting. While most good leading indicators work in a remarkably consistent way across space and time, they have all failed, on occasion, to anticipate a turn. This fact is an important caution for those who are inclined to rely on a single favorite indicator to monitor the economy.

For example, stock prices are widely considered to be a leading indicator of recession and recovery. In 2001, however, the market actually rallied as the recession began; the market anticipated a recovery and plummeted when the hopes proved unfounded.

Furthermore, falling stock prices often have many crying "recession" even when other indicators are healthy, as we saw after the stock market crash of 1987. As the well-known economist Paul Samuelson once quipped, the stock market has predicted nine of the last five recessions—hardly a reliable indicator on its own.

The growth rate cycle, however, is important. There is a one-to-one correspondence between growth rate cycles and stock price cycles. Predicting turns in the growth rate cycle, while not useful for anticipating recessions and recoveries, is important to equity investors in evaluating the movement of the market. It is also useful for many companies, where the difference between a rising and a falling rate of growth could make a major difference in forward planning.

Another well-known leading indicator is the yield curve, whose inversion—when short-term interest rates rise above long-term interest rates—is one of the best predictors of recessions. The yield curve, however, failed to properly invert ahead of the 1990–91 recession. In other words, it is important to know that on occasion some of the indicators that usually lead the business cycle may fail to do so.

THE COMPOSITE INDEX APPROACH

Fortunately, there is a solution to the problem of leading indicators that occasionally run off course. Over the decades we have observed that most leading indicators are unlikely to fail at the same time. At any given turn, some of them may miss the mark, but the majority of them will remain on track. Collectively, they cover for each other and provide the opportunity to make predictions that are consistently accurate. In the same way that you can diversify your portfolio with many different kinds of investments, you can reduce the risk of a bad forecast by using multiple indicators.

The vetting process we use for each indicator is exhaustive. Through decades of work, theories of the relationships that drive the business cycle have been posited and tested. A hundred indicators might be considered in order to come up with a handful that are reliable. Although any one of those will fail on occasion, collectively we've found they will succeed.

> ## The First Leading Indicators
> 1. Sensitive Commodity Prices
> 2. Average Workweek (Manufacturing)
> 3. Commercial and Industrial Building Contracts
> 4. New Incorporations
> 5. New Orders
> 6. Housing Starts
> 7. Stock Price Index
> 8. Business Failure Liabilities
>
> ECRI's founder, Dr. Geoffrey Moore, established the first list of leading economic indicators of recession and recovery in 1950.

In order to distill the message of the indicators, we combine them into a single summary measure. One difficulty in doing this is that it essentially involves combining apples and oranges. For example, how do you add up or balance out overtime hours and corporate bond yields? To get the most out of the indicators, it is necessary, in a sense, to make fruit juice.

In the late 1950s, Geoffrey Moore and his colleagues developed just such a breakthrough approach—a statistical tool known as a composite index.[1] The idea behind the composite index is that the common denominator of various cyclical indicators could be based on their sensitivity to the business cycle. Some indicators are extremely sensitive and move up and down a great deal before recessions and recoveries, such as stock prices. Others, like the average workweek, are less sensitive, but even the small movements they exhibit are significant. Looking at indicators in terms of their relative sensitivity to the cycle provides a common dimension on which they can be combined. This was the approach he used to develop the Index of Leading Economic Indicators (LEI).

Forty years later, the creation of the LEI remains a landmark accomplishment. But in terms of our ability to predict turning points, the state of the art has advanced considerably. The innovations reflected a more sophisticated understanding of the cyclical nature of the economy. From that expanded body of knowledge, we have developed forecasting tools that leave the LEI far behind.

It is not without nostalgia that we look back on Moore's pioneering work. But the demand for better forecasting compelled

How the Leading Indicators Compare

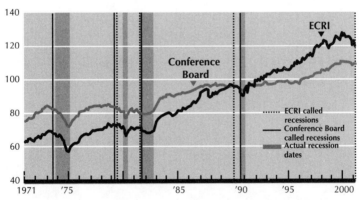

Note: Conference Board calls were not made at the time, but rather they would have called a recession based on a standard they've created since the last recession; ECRI did not make recession calls prior to 1979.

Sources: Economic Cycle Research Institute; The Conference Board

This chart ran in the Wall Street Journal *on April 19, 2001, comparing ECRI's Weekly Leading Index with the Index of Leading Economic Indicators (LEI, maintained by the Conference Board). ECRI forecast that a recession was unavoidable, while the LEI indicated that the expansion would continue.*

us to move forward. The Model T Ford represented cutting-edge technology in 1908, and remains highly valued by car aficionados. Still, nobody would rely on one today to make an important trip. Similarly, depending on the LEI to predict turning points has proved dangerous. In fact, the LEI failed to predict the last two U.S. recessions in real time, while ECRI's Weekly Leading Index (WLI), which we will soon discuss in detail, was right on target.[2]

Since the original LEI was put together, we have made substantial progress in composite index construction and in cyclical forecasting in general. Those advances are rooted in a broad observation of cycles wherever they exist, often in places no one looked before. To understand the foundation for these improvements, we must step back from a U.S.-centric view and examine business cycles around the world.

Our International Experience

6

The creation of the Index of Leading Economic Indicators (LEI) was a big step forward in the effort to predict turns in the U.S. business cycle. But Geoffrey Moore knew that in order to understand business cycles fully, they must be observed everywhere they occur. Were the sequences of events that transpired around turns in the U.S. business cycle also present in international economies?

To answer that question, Moore embarked on an ambitious expansion of business cycle research in the early 1970s. He and his colleagues began to develop leading indicators for other economies in order to better understand and test the circumstances in which they worked or failed.

Moore's NBER colleague, Philip Klein (now at ECRI), did much of the initial footwork. He spent a year in Europe, visiting various government statistical agencies to gather data. Since all nations' economies, not to mention their statistical collection methods, vary considerably, the data Klein gathered would have seemed incongruous to a casual observer. But using their experience—specifically, with the U.S. leading and coincident indicators as a guide—Moore and Klein identified analogous measures in order to test whether business cycles abroad followed patterns similar to those of the U.S. economy. Initially, Moore and Klein were interested in the world's major developed economies.

They found that in country after country, from the U.K. to West Germany, from Australia to Japan, the indicators showed that the business cycle's durable sequences held true. Their evidence belied the popular belief that each economy was unique— that a set of leading indicators that worked for one country would not work for another.

As news of their work spread, Moore and Klein received requests from other countries in Europe and Asia to help develop their own leading indicators. From 1979 to 1995, Moore's Center for International Business Cycle Research (CIBCR) studied international economies and developed leading indexes in collaboration with governments, central banks, and statistical agencies around the world.

In 1987, researchers from the University of Kiev approached CIBCR to investigate if leading indicators could be developed for the Soviet economy. Moore doubted that business cycles would be found in the Soviet Union's state-controlled economy. The business cycle is a product of the countless economic choices made in the free market. In the Soviet Union's centralized system of decision making, five-year economic plans dictated shifts in production, prices, employment, and income. Moore felt it was extremely unlikely that the cyclical forces characteristic of a free market would be relevant.

The Soviet Union's interest in our research was likely linked to President Mikhail Gorbachev's desire to reform communism. Gorbachev had always been fascinated with what he considered to be President Franklin D. Roosevelt's success in rescuing capitalism from its own Achilles' heel—the boom-bust cycle that in the 1930s culminated in the Great Depression. Like FDR, Gorbachev wanted to save his country's economy from the system's inherent weaknesses without discarding its basic tenets.

As Moore expected, leading indicators failed completely in the Soviet Union. While limited fluctuations were seen in their data, they were due in large part to international cycles transmitted through trade. Essentially, there was no business cycle to predict in the communist Soviet economy.

A similar exercise was undertaken with the Central Bank of Jordan, whose economy had historically suffered large fluctuations. The leading indicators that worked in so many other free-market economies failed to "lead" in Jordan. Why? we wondered. Jordan's economic fluctuations, we discovered, were driven by Mideast conflicts and political crises. In other words, the overwhelming drivers of its economic cycle were war and peace rather than free-market forces. As a result, the business cycle forces were subverted.

Interestingly, more than a decade later, in 1998, Jordan's central bank, under a new governor, asked ECRI to help build an indicator system for their economy. We reminded them that we had tried years before and found the effort to be futile. But they assured us that their economy had changed in the interim now that war and politics were less dominant features. And sure enough, when we revisited the earlier indicators, we found that they had begun to work quite well.

Working on economic indicators for India provided us with another lesson in predicting cycles. The 1990–91 Gulf Crisis had a little-known effect on the Indian economy. As a result of the conflict, Indian expatriates working in Kuwait, Iraq, and other countries in the region were forced to leave. Suddenly, the inflow of money from the expatriate workers stopped. India's foreign-exchange reserves plunged, and the country found itself in a full-scale economic crisis. In response, the newly elected Indian government began to liberalize the economy, allowing the influence of the free market to grow.

Before 1991, the leading indicators of the business cycle had failed to accurately predict the direction of the Indian economy because of large distortions of the free-market system (as well as a significant level of central planning). Pre-1991, the Indian economy was a hybrid. Although the private sector flourished, it existed alongside a state-controlled economy. More than half of economic capital was controlled by the government. Five-year economic plans dictated major investments. Almost everything that was bought and sold domestically had some sort of price distortion—through subsidies, price ceilings, or the full-scale licensing of industries.

The pre-1991 Indian economy did experience some economic ups and downs, but these cycles were driven by monsoons more than anything else. If the monsoon failed, droughts were severe and agricultural production plunged. This plunge would reverberate throughout the rest of the economy in the months that followed. The free market took a back seat; the best way to predict the economy was to follow the weather.

But after the early 1990s, as economic liberalization took hold—including the removal of many price controls and licensing requirements—those same indicators started to work, correctly predicting turns in the cycle.

In addition to India's economic liberalization, there had been an evolution in terms of India's dependence on agriculture. In the

Growth Rates (%) of Indian Long Leading and Coincident Indexes, 1977–2000

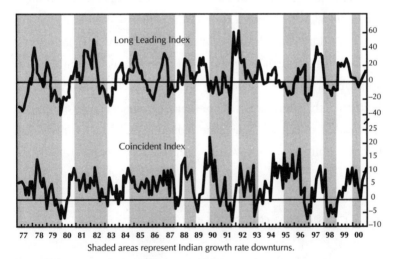

77 78 79 80 81 82 83 84 85 86 87 88 89 90 91 92 93 94 95 96 97 98 99 00

Shaded areas represent Indian growth rate downturns.

The Indian Long Leading Index was unable to call turns in the economy before the 1990s. But after free-market forces were unleashed, the Long Leading Index began to perform quite well. Notice how that index turns ahead of shaded areas marking off cyclical turns.

1960s and 1970s, close to half of India's GDP was related to agriculture. By the late 1990s, this dependence had dropped to only one quarter. Advancements in irrigation reduced the likelihood of drought in case of a failure of the monsoon, and India had begun to build up stocks of food grains to prevent shortages when crops failed. As a result, the economy's vulnerability to monsoons decreased significantly. More important, the liberalization of the economy meant that India was acting more like a free market. Now the fundamental drivers of the business cycle were freed up, and the cyclical forces measured by leading indicators emerged as key drivers of the economy.

Some wondered whether our indicators would hold up in South Africa in the wake of the dismantling of apartheid. Earlier, although apartheid was the major feature of the political system, the economy was dominated by a free market and the cyclical indicators worked. After apartheid ended, the Reserve Bank of South Africa approached us about reviewing our findings. Did our indicators hold up in the aftermath of major structural change? We found that they did. The fact that the same indicators worked in drastically different political systems was another testament to their durability.

THE DANGERS OF DATA FITTING

The success of leading indicators in market economies encouraged many countries to try to adapt them to fit local conditions. The problem is that many economists tend to create models or simplified representations of the economy that assume recent trends will continue into the future—a surefire recipe for missing a turning point. In some countries, economists took better-known leading indicators of the business cycle and made simplifying assumptions to argue that their models now incorporated cyclical risks. In other countries, economists insisted that because the structure of their economy differed from that of the United States, different indicators would be needed to predict their business cycles.

There is some truth to the latter idea. But the tendency to use simplified models based on past data inevitably led to glaring failures in recession forecasting. The Organization for Economic Cooperation and Development (OECD) helps each member country select indicators for its own economy, based in part on what local economists feel would work best given the unique circumstances of their own country. Yet these indicators seldom work (actually they seem to work in retrospect, but mostly because the OECD revises the trends in hindsight). A South Korean delegate, for example, reported at an OECD meeting in 1996 that the South Korean government's leading index, developed based on its ability to "predict" past turns in the economic cycle, failed to anticipate future turns. To correct this, the indicators were repeatedly refitted to include the new turning point data, only to fail again at a subsequent turning point. The delegate asked, "What good are leading indicators if they predict only past turning points?"

It was exactly the outcome that Moore had warned of. Some indicators might seem to provide a good fit for specific countries for a period of time, but the question was whether those indicators could accurately predict future turning points. He believed that the drivers of the business cycle should be the fundamental guideline in the selection of indicators, no matter what economy was being examined. Our own South Korean leading indexes have predicted turning points there well, precisely because they do not reflect the limited circumstances of a particular time and place.

But while the principal drivers of the business cycle—like profits and inventories—remain the basis for accurate indicators in every country we examined, it was sometimes difficult to find suitable measures of those drivers. Frequently, the data in a country would be unreliable or biased in some manner.

For example, when we began working with Mexico's central bank in 1998 to develop a cyclical monitoring system, we used the jobless rate as a coincident indicator to help establish the business cycle chronology. Going back to the 1980s, the Mexican jobless rate occasionally fell as low as 2 percent. This ran against our understanding of the extent of joblessness in the Mexican economy. When we investigated further, we found that the jobless data were strongly biased by local definitions of joblessness. In Mexico, if a person had done any kind of work, loosely defined, in the last twelve months, he or she was considered employed. Clearly, many "unemployed" people fit this classification.

Although this made the Mexican jobless data unsuitable for many forecasting models, we were able to use the data anyway. The number itself was biased, and the actual level of unemployment was undoubtedly much higher. But the timing of the cyclical turns in the data confirmed the timing found in other coincident measures of the business cycle, such as production and sales. Although biased, the relative rise and fall of the unemployment figures worked just fine for our purposes in identifying and predicting the timing of economic turning points.

The United States, relatively speaking, has some of the world's best data, yet economists here, too, sometimes attribute their forecasting failures to data inaccuracies. For example, until revisions in late July 2002 showed that U.S. GDP had declined in the first three quarters of 2001 rather than in just the third quarter, many prominent economists who had failed to predict the 2001 recession continued to claim there had been no recession at all. When they finally faced the truth that they had been wrong, they blamed it on bad data.

In developing countries where data are often sparse and flawed, the problem is worse. This makes it difficult to build forecasting models that rely on high data quality in order to work properly. Quite often, these are also the economies that can least afford the time, money, and effort needed to build a world-class system of statistical data collection. The lack of high-quality data in developing countries poses major problems for standard model-based approaches to forecasting. But, as the example of Mexico illustrates, when the focus is primarily on identifying turning points in the cycle, the knowledge of indicators that turn in durable sequences in country after country is invaluable in identifying the right selection of leading indicators.

AN ANSWER TO MEASUREMENT WITHOUT THEORY

In the mid-1990s, Moore and his colleague John Cullity (who also helped establish ECRI) updated Moore's 1950 study of the leading indicators of revival and recession. Moore's original study had examined U.S. data from 1870 to 1938, and his eight original leading indicators of revival and recession (see table on

Lead/Lag Record of Eight Leading Indicators in the United States and Abroad

Average Lead (–) or Lag (+) in Months

Indicators	At Peaks			At Troughs		
	U.S. before 1938	U.S. 1948–1991	10 Other Countries 1948–1987	U.S. before 1938	U.S. 1948–1991	10 Other Countries 1948–1987
1. Sensitive Commodity Prices	–2	–4	–2	–1	+2	+1
2. Average Workweek (Mfg.)	–3	–6	–4	–3	–1	–4
3. Commercial and Industrial Building Contracts	–3	–6	–1	–1	+2	0
4. New Incorporations	–3	–7	–8	–4	–4	–8
5. New Orders	–4	–6	–6	–2	–1	–9
6. Housing Starts	–6	–12	–6	–4	–5	–7
7. Stock Price Index	–6	–6	–6	–6	–5	–7
8. Business Failure Liabilities	–9	–10	n.a.	–8	–1	n.a.
Average, 7 Indicators	–4	–7	–5	–3	–2	–5
Average, 8 Indicators	–4	–7	n.a.	–4	–2	n.a.

The figures represent the lead time in months that the indicators had in predicting turns in the economy. In such predictions, minus signs are what forecasters look for—they show that the indicators lead the economy rather than follow it. As you can see, the original eight U.S. leading indicators selected in 1950 continue to work, both in the United States and abroad.

page 94) had been chosen in part on the basis of their performance over that period. They tested these eight original indicators to see whether they had worked in the United States, as well as in ten other countries around the world, during the second half of the twentieth century.

And they did. The same fundamental drivers of the business cycle spanned an economy all the way from buggy whips of the nineteenth century to computer chips of the twentieth. And those drivers worked just as well in late-twentieth-century South Korea, Germany, and New Zealand as they did in post–Civil War United States.

The essential common thread among those radically different societies and technological eras was the free market itself. The business cycle theory broke down only where the market was not truly free because of central planning, or because it was overwhelmed by war, weather, or political upheaval.

Moore and Cullity published their findings in a 1994 paper[1] called "An Answer to Measurement Without Theory." The indicators had been chosen with a strong appreciation for the drivers of the business cycle, and they had proved durable across time and space. The theory underlying the choice of leading indicators had been validated.

The work on cyclical indicators has been perhaps the longest-standing experiment in economics. From mid-nineteenth-century America to late-twentieth-century Taiwan, the same durable sequences of leading, lagging, and coincident indicators had been shown to work wherever the free market reigned.

The lessons of the business cycle, however, were drowned out by the sheer noise of the bull-market party that was raging during the late 1990s. The fact that durable sequences characterized cyclical turns in every market economy meant little to those climbing the peak of the latest New Economy. From those giddy heights, nothing learned from past observation seemed relevant. The old rules no longer applied. This time, things were different. Or so the pundits said. It would take a bust that stripped away trillions of dollars to prove that thinking wrong.

Measuring
Business Cycles:
The State of the Art

O f course, there is more to any economy than a single over-arching business cycle. In fact, it is simplistic to think that any one leading index can capture all of the ebbs and flows in an economy. Geoffrey Moore's observations revealed that, beneath the overall business cycle, there were a number of loosely related but distinct cycles at work.

As it turns out, it is absolutely essential to be able to predict the direction of these "many cycles," not so much as a way to predict turns in the overall business cycle but to avoid being misled by seemingly contradictory evidence. For example, in Chapter 4 we discussed how the late-1990s bubble economy was encouraged by a misunderstanding of the link between economic growth and inflation, which fueled misguided exuberance about a "new paradigm" of endless noninflationary growth. But if you were watching the Future Inflation Gauge, or FIG, it was clear that this was just a temporary delinking of cycles in inflation and growth. To the surprise of many, but in line with the FIG, the Federal Reserve raised interest rates aggressively in 1999–2000, triggering a bear market in bonds and ultimately popping the bubble. This gives you a taste of how powerful the many-cycles view can be.

The 2001 recession brought with it correct predictions of a downturn in inflation, but even louder calls that the housing "bubble" would soon burst. Once again, confounding the experts, home prices didn't follow the course of overall inflation. In fact, as our Leading Home Price Index predicted, home prices kept rising through the recession and recovery.

Or think of the "jobless recoveries" that followed the business cycle upturns in 1991 and 2001. Understanding that the cycles in employment are different from the business cycle, and using our Leading Employment Index to separately assess job prospects, provided clues to the gloomy employment outlook despite a clear upturn in GDP growth. Thus, following these many cycles can help you foresee when the behavior of the economy will depart from the norm propounded by the pundits. For investors, the best opportunities are often created by such divergences, which blindside even sophisticated financial professionals.

For businesses, the nuances revealed by the many-cycles view are also critical. For example, in a two-speed economy, an accurate forecast of a U.S. business cycle upswing may be accompanied by weakness in global manufacturing, as was the case following the 1997 Asian Crisis. Without the Leading Manufacturing Index to highlight the gloom in the industrial sector, a manufacturing firm could well be misled by correctly optimistic predictions about the overall business cycle. Analogous situations could arise for companies in construction or services, where growth may be temporarily out of sync with the overall economy.

For investment professionals, of course, early warning of such divergences between sectors can be invaluable for guiding asset allocation. For businesses and individuals alike, the many-cycles view reduces the apparent discord in the deluge of data, clarifying the complexities of the economy and providing clear clues to the correct course of action.

In short, the research done in the decades since Moore created the first leading economic index is a powerful complement to our international work and ultimately gave us a much richer and more nuanced cyclical worldview. The extensions of the basic leading index approach were both extensive (looking at cycles in other market economies) and intensive (examining the many cycles within each country's economy). The fruition of that research resulted in a comprehensive framework for measuring business cycles that took the state of the art well beyond the popularly perceived limits of economic cycle forecasting.

PREDICTING CYCLES IN INFLATION

In a sense, our many-cycles investigation harked back to the early days of the NBER and its work on inflation cycles. Over centuries, price levels have always been cyclical, rising and falling without changing much over the long term. But in the early 1930s, the behavior of prices shifted. Before then, it was not unusual to see a decline in general price levels during downturns. After 1932, they just kept going up.

This change in price patterns coincided with the lower volatility of the business cycle following World War II. As we saw with the taming of the cycle in Chapter 3, the rise of the service sector reduced price volatility because inventory cycles were no longer a dominant factor. Automatic stabilizers such as unemployment insurance ensured that price levels would not fall very much. Additionally, increased government spending contributed to a general tendency toward inflation while smoothing out the cycle. In some ways, it seemed as if the cost of taming the cycle was inflation.

Moore recognized that even if price levels themselves had become less cyclical, the growth rate of prices—that is, inflation—remained quite cyclical. In other words, cycles in the rate of inflation were very much alive.

For students of the business cycle, this was no revelation. But something unusual happened to the economy during the 1970s. Conventional wisdom held that economic growth and inflation were closely linked, with inflation following economic growth up and down. After a slowdown or a recession, inflation had always dropped. After a pickup in growth, inflation had risen. But the 1970s was a period characterized by persistently high inflation *and* persistently weak growth. The phenomenon known as "stagflation" demonstrated that cycles in economic growth and inflation could sometimes have distinctly different timing— with rising inflation coexisting with falling growth.

For forecasters, this meant that economic growth could not always be used to predict inflation. Still, to this day, many continue to forecast inflation this way.

The practice of linking growth to inflation is a classic example of the problems that can arise when the economy is viewed through too narrow a lens. If you looked only at economic activity and inflation through the 1960s, it would seem as if growth and inflation were closely linked. Observing growth and inflation just during the late 1970s, however, might have led one to conclude just the opposite. Inflation downswings follow slowdowns in growth about 70 percent of the time. But 30 percent of the time inflation declines *before* growth turns down. (There are also times, like the late 1970s, when inflation and economic growth appear to delink.) The timing relationship between cycles in growth and inflation is more complicated than most would suspect without longer-term study into the drivers of inflation cycles. Such findings underscore the importance of observing extensively first and theorizing later.

Moore decided that inflation cycles warranted separate study. He examined the empirical evidence to see what happened in reality, and casting a wide net, took clues from a variety of sources—including employment data, monetary measures, and international trade—to create a set of leading indicators of inflation. He then combined these indicators into a composite index, which marked the genesis of what has become known as the Future Inflation Gauge, or FIG, designed to measure underlying inflationary pressures.

There is good reason for the FIG to be held in such high esteem. Taken alone, leading indexes of growth could not predict stagflation; they are designed only to predict business cycles. But inflation forecasting based on economic growth turned out to be as unreliable in the 1990s as it was in the 1970s. In the latter part of the long expansion of the 1990s, inflation and economic activity once again

Future Inflation Gauge and CPI Inflation

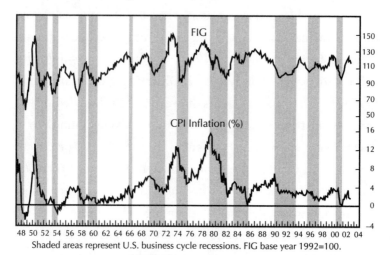

Shaded areas represent U.S. business cycle recessions. FIG base year 1992=100.

The FIG turns up and down ahead of upswings and downswings in inflation. The shaded bars show the inflation downswings.

delinked, but in the opposite direction, as the economy experienced strong inflation-free growth.

Some could explain this phenomenon only by invoking a "new paradigm"—the old economic rules had changed, they claimed. Many economists credited growth without inflation to the "productivity miracle" made possible by tremendous advancements in information technology. It was a classic example of the tendency to find an explanation to fit a narrow set of circumstances. While events temporarily supported these conclusions, they ultimately proved insufficient. Even researchers from the Federal Reserve supported some of the New Economy claims, but when inflation pressures rose in 1999, shown by the FIG, the Fed did not hesitate to raise interest rates aggressively.

Without invoking any new paradigm to explain the divergence between growth and inflation, ECRI's separate leading indicators of growth and inflation correctly predicted the apparent anomaly of strong noninflationary growth from 1996 to 1999. It was a powerful demonstration of the value offered by a many-cycles approach to forecasting.

CYCLES IN EMPLOYMENT

Employment, like inflation, is related to cycles in economic growth, but it too can diverge from economic growth at turning points. Generally speaking, employment tends to peak just before the overall economy does and trough slightly afterward. But this is not a fixed relationship: The period of time between related turns can vary significantly. Sometimes the lag is short, as in the case of a strong, or "V-shaped," recovery (as in 1982–83). And sometimes the lag is long, like the weak or "jobless" recoveries that followed the 1990–91 and 2001 recessions.

Therefore, in order to determine the current state of the employment cycle and forecast its course, a separate set of indicators is needed. Moore first considered what drove the employment cycle. He then selected potential leading indicators, tested them empirically, and devised a set of coincident and leading indexes of employment. For example, nonfarm payroll jobs is a good coincident employment indicator, while initial jobless claims is a good leading employment indicator. Decades ago, such thinking revealed gaps in the type of data collected. During his term as Commissioner of Labor Statistics in Washington, Moore convinced the government to collect additional statistics,

U.S. Leading and Coincident Employment Indexes

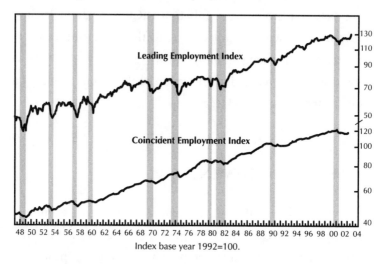

Index base year 1992=100.

The Leading Employment Index turns up and down ahead of upswings and downswings in employment, tracked by the Coincident Employment Index. Here the shaded bars show business cycle recessions.

such as the Employment Cost Index, which, three decades later, remains a popular measure among analysts.

As a result of these efforts, we now had a more sophisticated three-dimensional view of the economy. Looking at employment, inflation, and economic growth individually reveals a dynamic and complex system that is otherwise hidden from view.

The various cycle peaks and troughs do not occur in a set sequence, but shift about like a series of moving targets. Inflation, employment, and economic growth actually represent three separate "aspects" of the economy.

CYCLES WITHIN GROWTH: FOREIGN TRADE

In an era of increased globalization, foreign trade has become a major influence on the domestic economy. As free trade grew in the late twentieth century, it became clear that a sound knowledge of the cycles in imports and exports was important for accurate forecasting.

Exports are driven by two basic factors: first, the state of the trading partners' economies; and second, price competitiveness, as determined by the currency exchange rate. Thus, our long leading indexes of growth for most industrialized nations can be used in conjunction with exchange rates to predict cycles in exports. For example, if the long leading indexes for the major trading partners of the United States were to strengthen while the value of the dollar remained stable, then U.S. exports would climb faster. If the dollar also weakened, exports would soar. Similarly, by using domestic leading indexes and exchange rates, cyclical moves in imports can be also be predicted. Adding up the forecasts for exports and imports gives us a view of where the trade balance is headed.

Trade flows can also be looked at from the point of view of another country, such as Germany or Japan, or even developing countries, like India, that are growing in importance and where good economic indicators are scarce.[1] In each case, a number of different cycles are required to complete the picture.

Key to an ongoing research program is the focus on the discovery of new relationships. While the creation of the original leading index was a good first step, it was not sufficient to capture the full complexity of the U.S. economy. It turned out that the economy was marching to the beat of many different drummers.

LONG AND SHORT LEADING INDICATORS

As we continued to research leading indicators of the overall economy, it became apparent that some indicators had long leads and others had short leads. With an upturn approaching, the longer leading indicators would begin to turn up in anticipation. The shorter leading indicators, however, would not yet foresee the turning point, so they would continue on a downward track. Since some indicators were going up and others were still going down, their signals risked canceling each other out as turns approached. These cross-currents in the components made it more difficult to predict turning points.

We found that the long and short leading indicators provide clearer signals if they are separated into distinct indexes so that they can be watched sequentially. In that way, the long leading index would begin to move first, signaling that we were approaching a turning point in the economy. That signal would be confirmed when the short leading index began to move. This approach *does* work in the real world, and has given us clear signals of approaching turning points over the past two decades.

The long leading index can accurately signal a turn in the economy up to one year in advance. Such a long lead time gives us earlier warning. The short leading index begins to turn six months or so before a downturn. It both confirms the signal of

U.S. Long Leading, Short Leading, and Coincident Indexes

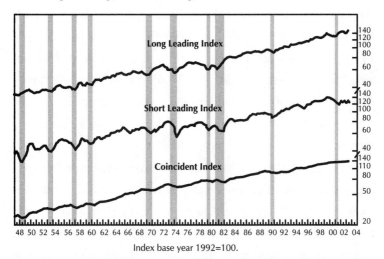

Index base year 1992=100.

The Long Leading, Short Leading, and Coincident Indexes typically turn up and down in sequence. The Long Leading Index gives the earliest warning of recessions, the Short Leading Index confirms this signal, and the Coincident Index then declines during the recession, shown by the shaded bars. The same sequence is followed before a recovery.

the long leading index and provides added focus and conviction as the decision point approaches.

To help monitor developments on a more frequent basis, Moore helped develop a Weekly Leading Index (WLI) in 1983. Some of the components of the WLI, like initial jobless claims, had long been available on a weekly basis. Others had to be created from scratch, like the *Journal of Commerce*–ECRI industrial materials price index, designed to measure inflation in a broad range of industrial raw materials.

Starting in 1983, the weekly index was published in *Business-Week* magazine. Known at the time as the *BusinessWeek* Leading Index, it correctly predicted the 1990–91 recession and recovery. In the late 1990s, ECRI began to publish the index through our website, businesscycle.com. In 2001, the WLI again turned down well before the economy did,[2] and it also predicted the subsequent recovery while many were fearful of a double-dip recession.

Typically, all three of these indexes turn in sequence. On average, the long leader provides signals a year in advance, the weekly leader ten months in advance, and the short leader six months in advance of a recession. Thus, we now monitor the evolution of the overall economic cycle much more closely and accurately than ever before.

Weekly Leading Index

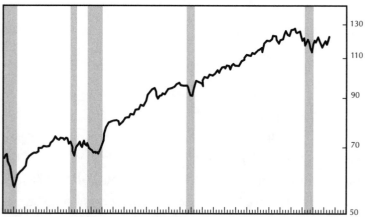

Shaded areas represent U.S. business cycle recessions. Index base year 1992=100.

The Weekly Leading Index turns down before recessions, shown by the shaded bars, and turns up before the recessions end.

CYCLES IN SEGMENTS OF THE ECONOMY

A closer look at broad sectors within the overall economy is often critical for businesses that cater to specific industries, and for investment professionals who have to assess the relative strength of different sectors. If this does not sound like you, feel free to skip ahead to the next section.

The manufacturing and service sectors, for example, behave quite differently from one another. While loosely related to the overall economy, their individual cycles are distinct enough to be worthy of separate sets of indicators, because they could, and on occasion do, turn at different times.

U.S. Services and Manufacturing Leading and Coincident Indexes, Growth Rates (%)

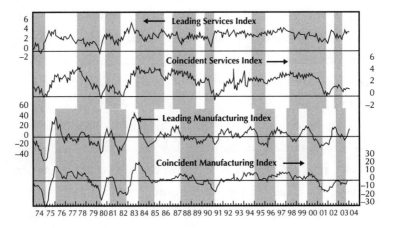

The shaded areas in the upper panel show downturns in service sector growth, while those in the lower panel show downturns in manufacturing growth. Notice that they are not in sync. Therefore, it is helpful to have separate leading indexes for services and manufacturing.

A downturn in one sector does not necessarily mean that other sectors will turn down, as we saw with the "two-speed economy" of the late 1990s. In the wake of the Asian Crisis, manufacturing entered a sharp downturn but the service sector did not. As a result, the overall economy continued to grow even while layoffs and cutbacks in production were gathering steam in manufacturing.

For many decision makers, the performance of one sector is much more important than another. An employee or manager in financial services needs specific information about cycles in that sector to make good choices. An investor needs to know whether the direction of earnings in a sector is likely to shift. A central banker might want to assess whether inflation pressures are heating up.

ECRI monitors cycles in the services, manufacturing, and construction sectors, as well as in the financial services subsector. In the early 1990s, we helped create the U.S. government's leading indexes of primary metals, which are maintained by the U.S. Geological Survey.[3] In addition, we can monitor cycles within specific regions, as we have done for New York City and the state of Connecticut.

We have also developed leading indexes for specific industries. The dominant companies in any given industry often have distinct product lines that are sensitive to cyclical swings in demand. By combining national economic data with industry- and company-specific data, we have successfully developed indicators that can predict swings in industry demand and prices. This information, coupled with our other indexes, has proven quite valuable in decision making.

We have created another index that should benefit virtually all readers at some time in their lives. The Leading Home Price Index (LHPI) provides a cyclical view of home prices within the overall inflation cycle. Home prices are not just an important aspect of the national economy; they also represent the largest single investment decision most individuals make. The 2001 recession demonstrated the LHPI's value. Typically, home prices have experienced a cyclical decline around the time of a downturn in the economic cycle. In 2001, because of favorable demographics and falling interest rates, home prices actually rose during the recession. The LHPI correctly anticipated that prices would hold up when most forecasters were confident that a plunge in home prices was imminent. Clearly, the LHPI can be an important tool in making a decision about when to buy—or sell—a home.

U.S. Leading Home Price Index and Real Home Prices

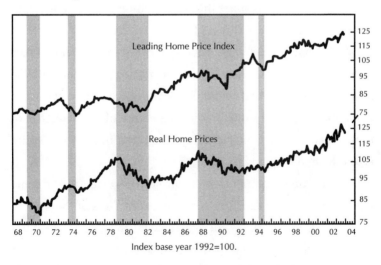

Index base year 1992=100.

The Leading Home Price Index turns up and down before upswings and downswings in inflation-adjusted home prices. Home price downturns are marked by the shaded bars.

The many-cycles view of the economy lies at the core of the economic dashboard described in Chapters 8 and 9. But the next step is to pull all of these indexes together into an easy-to-use framework.

The state of the art in forecasting is never static. After all, our own view of the economy has evolved significantly as the body of business cycle research continues to grow. The many-cycles view pushed us deeper into the nature of business cycles, leading to more sophisticated forecasting tools. Without such advancements, it would have been difficult, if not impossible, for us to predict the recession of 2001.

TODAY'S STATE OF THE ART

How is it possible to apply the basic leading index approach in forecasting to all these different aspects of the economy? Fortunately, the many cycles we have described exhibit similar key characteristics. First, they share the principle of the durable sequence, meaning that economic events move in a known order at turning points. It is the predictable nature of this sequence of events that allows us to forecast cycle turns in both the entire economy and its many parts.

Second, their turning points can be recognized in the same way. Specifically, at each turning point, regardless of the kind of cycle we are monitoring—the aggregate business cycle, the inflation cycle, or the specialized sectoral cycles—the indexes, in order to signal a genuine turn in the cycle, must change direction in a way that is *pronounced, pervasive,* and *persistent.* We call this "the three P's."

Why are the three P's so important? When a leading index forecasts a change in the direction of the cycle in a pronounced, pervasive, and persistent manner, the likelihood of a turn rises significantly. We will illustrate these concepts with charts showing a three P's analysis of the Leading Employment Index at the time ECRI made its 2001 recession call.

Pervasiveness measures the extent to which the economy as a whole is affected by the cycle. During a cyclical upswing the improvement in economic activity spreads from one company to another, from one industry to another, and from one region to another. These developments multiply throughout the economy as an expansion takes hold. In the case of a contraction, the downturn also spreads out across industries and regions. *Pervasive* movement

How Pervasive a Decline in Leading Employment Index Growth?

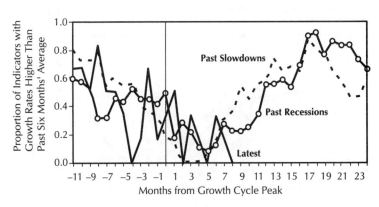

This chart shows the proportion of Leading Employment Index components that have improved over the past six months' average. The pattern in the 2001 cycle is overlaid on the patterns seen at the same stage in past cycles. This way we can see whether the latest cycle is closer to a recession pattern or a slowdown pattern.

is revealed by watching the percentage of components contributing to an index's rise or fall and comparing that pattern with past cycles (see chart on previous page).

A cyclical change also needs to be *pronounced*—of sufficient magnitude—in order to distinguish it from mere fluctuations or "noise." As a directional change in growth becomes more pervasive, it begins to snowball, gaining momentum and magnitude, becoming more pronounced. Again, in order to get a sense of just how pronounced a movement is, one needs to compare it with past cycles (see chart below).

Finally, the cyclical movement must be *persistent* in order to qualify as a cyclical upswing or downswing, because such a move feeds on itself, prolonging the move. A slowdown in sales may cause a production cutback, triggering job losses and low-

How Pronounced a Decline in Leading Employment Index Growth?

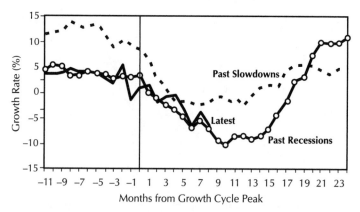

This chart shows the growth rate of the Leading Employment Index, with the pattern in the 2001 cycle overlaid on the patterns seen at the same stage in past cycles. Again, we can see whether the latest cycle is closer to a recession pattern or a slowdown pattern.

ering incomes, which in turn feeds back again to even lower sales, creating a vicious cycle. Just a month or two of movement may indicate nothing more than an economic hiccup. A move in cyclical indicators that is somewhat pervasive and pronounced does not qualify as a cyclical turn if it lasts only a couple of months. Technically, a cyclical upswing or downswing has to persist for at least five months in order to be labeled as such. Most last much longer (see chart below).

These two characteristics, the durable sequence and the three P's, are common to all cycles, whether in overall economic activity, inflation, employment, economic sectors, or foreign trade. These similarities allowed us to develop forecasting tools that share a consistent design while complementing each other.

How Persistent a Decline in Leading Employment Index Growth?

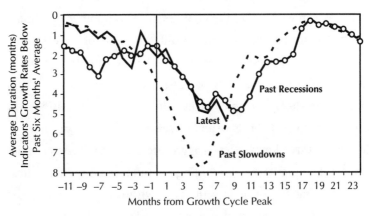

This chart shows how long on average the Leading Employment Index components have been declining. The pattern in the 2001 cycle is overlaid on the patterns seen at the same stage in past cycles. This way we can see whether the latest cycle is closer to a recession pattern or a slowdown pattern.

PUTTING IT ALL TOGETHER: THE ECRI CUBE

The economy is a highly complex system. But econometricians typically build models from equations that try to mimic the way it has moved in the past. Such models oversimplify the real world and fail to capture the complexity that produces economic fluctuations. The forecasting record shows that these models break down when they are needed most—at predicting turning points when the economy shifts directions and the rules of the game change.

We've shown that the economy's complexity cannot be captured in a single leading index. Our forecasting success comes from a many-cycles view that monitors events as they actually happen, tracking leading indicators to measure the risk of a directional change in many different aspects of the economy. Only in that way can we capture the nuances of the economy's gyrations.

The interrelationships among different parts of the economy are not static (as most econometric models assume) but dynamic, i.e., ever-shifting. The challenge of a many-cycles approach is in combining these multiple cycles into one coherent outlook. In order to accurately observe and forecast the economy, we need to follow its three key aspects—aggregate economic activity, inflation, and employment—including the numerous specific indicators tracking the durable sequences within those cycles. How can all of this be captured and monitored at one time?

In the last ten years, our observations have crystallized to form the multidimensional framework that we call the *economic cycle cube*. It gives us a representation of what is going on in the economy's complex organic system.

Economic activity, employment, and inflation form the three dimensions of the cube. We further divide economic activity into foreign trade and domestic activity. Finally, domestic activity is sliced up both by sector and by long and short leading indicators. In this way, the full array of leading indexes monitored at ECRI (more than 100 in all) can be organized to produce a coherent and evolving outlook.

To be sure, the majority of individuals and small businesses have no special need for such a sophisticated "dashboard." However, in working with global corporations and financial institutions, we have found that such a state-of-the-art cockpit can be useful (much as a commercial jetliner has a far more sophisticated array of instruments than does a single-propeller private airplane).

The Economic Cycle Cube

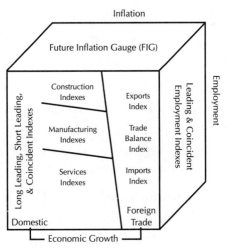

Three key aspects of the economy are shown—economic growth, inflation, and employment. The economic growth aspect is sliced up into areas covered by specialized leading indexes.

The cube construct enables ECRI to view growth and inflation in the economy independently, allowing us to see when they are moving in or out of sync. The cube also provides us with a mental framework for arranging and making sense of the constant flow of economic data that would be impossible to manage otherwise.

Each of our composite indexes organizes and distills data on a relatively small scale. But as the number of indexes increases with our many-cycles approach, it is necessary to create a larger framework to organize them all. Each month, as countless bits of economic data are produced worldwide, we focus on the data needed to update our indexes, then interpret their performance within the framework of the cube.

The cube represents the state of the art in economic cycle analysis in terms of the variety of leading indicators it allows us to analyze. But our knowledge keeps growing as we continue our research and observation. New cyclical relationships are sure to be discovered or come into greater focus as our understanding of the economy evolves. Our development of indicators for new countries will add levels of nuance and insight beyond our reach today. While we do not know exactly what shape the research will take in the future, we are establishing "cubes" with similar systematically interrelated parts for all the major economies in the world.

Both stagflation and inflation-free growth are hard for most economic models to predict, as they require modifications to standard economic theories. The cube does not require any modification in order to suggest a nonstandard economic outlook. Key aspects of the economy are placed in separate but loosely related dimensions, so there is no contradiction in forecasting cycles that

ECRI's International Coverage

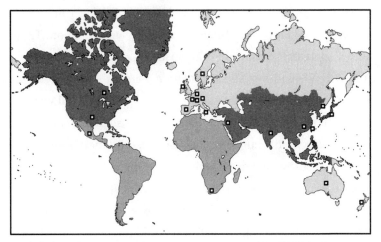

Each little cube represents an economy covered by ECRI indexes.

---

may or may not be in sync. While inflation-free growth and even two-speed economies may be unusual developments, they are entirely predictable when observed through the cube framework. Such powerful insights are invaluable when the consensus is confounded by divergences from standard models of the economy.

THE PROOF IS IN THE PUDDING

The cube's "many-cycles" perspective has proven its merit numerous times in recent years, allowing us to build a consistent track record of predictions. Standard econometric modeling approaches that many economists and businesses still follow are unable to duplicate our record. In recent years, economic growth, inflation, and employment cycles have sometimes operated out of sync, as they have on many occasions in the postwar era.

Employment declined in 1976 and 1978, for example, even though inflation continued to climb, creating what came to be known as stagflation—economic stagnation with inflation. There were also several episodes in the postwar era when employment grew strongly without causing inflation. Out of thirteen upswings in employment during the postwar period, ten were followed by an inflation upswing within a year or so. This emboldened some econometric model builders to assume that inflation *always* rises when the jobless rate drops below a threshold. However, in two cases, the inflation upswing started *before* the upswing in employment began, and in 1980, 1991, and 1996, a sustained upswing in employment was accompanied by an inflation *downturn*. Models that assumed stable links between unemployment and inflation proved inadequate for forecasting what happened during the late 1990s boom.

The cube's ability to see through the confusion has paid handsome dividends for those who followed our work. Five months before the start of the 1990–91 recession, ECRI's Leading Employment Index forecast a sharp, recessionary rise in the jobless rate. Combined with weakness in our leading indexes of growth, this made it clear that a recession was imminent. The recession of 1990–91 started in July 1990, but no one "predicted" it until well after the fact. When the recovery began in early 1991, most failed to note its arrival because the jobless rate kept rising even though economic activity, led by the service sector, was picking up—as anticipated by the Leading Services Index (see chart on facing page). Many companies missed the so-called jobless recovery because it looked like no recovery at all. Yet those who prepared for the upturn enjoyed a significant competitive advantage.

The cube also provided critical insights in the late 1990s,

U.S. Leading Services Index, Growth Rate (%)

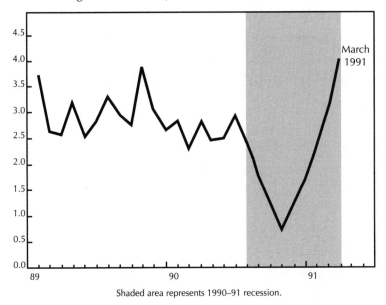

Shaded area represents 1990–91 recession.

Growth in the Leading Services Index anticipated the end of the 1991 recession.

when the U.S. economy experienced several years of strong non-inflationary growth. To explain this phenomenon many had to invoke a "new paradigm" of inflation-free growth. During this period, the Future Inflation Gauge (FIG) accurately predicted subdued inflation, even as our separate leading indicators of economic growth correctly forecast a robust economy. In other words, we did not need to create any new indexes to predict or explain these events—the ECRI cube had no problem predicting the phenomenon of inflation-free growth. Rather than credit a productivity miracle, we could see (through the FIG) that overall inflationary pressures were being kept in check primarily by falling import prices rather than New Economy productivity.

During that period, U.S. Federal Reserve policy correlated remarkably with cycles in the FIG. So it was not surprising that during congressional testimony Alan Greenspan said that he would look very closely at our inflation indicators.[4] A recent biography of Greenspan stated that the FIG is one of his favorite indicators.[5]

In 1997, one of the nation's largest mutual funds, which follows the ECRI cube closely, took particular interest in the plunge in our Japanese Long Leading Index of economic growth, which was predicting a new recession. It was not just the Japanese gov-

Future Inflation Gauge, Fed Funds Rate, and CPI Inflation, 1988–2001

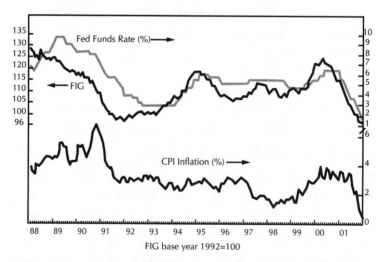

FIG base year 1992=100

During this period, when the Fed moved preemptively ahead of inflation, the Future Inflation Gauge anticipated the ups and downs in the Fed funds rate. Before the 1990–91 and 2001 recessions, which lowered inflation sharply, the Fed funds rate lagged noticeably behind the Future Inflation Gauge.

ernment that was oblivious to this threat, but Japanese businesses as well. In June 1997, three months into the new recession, the Bank of Japan's respected Tankan survey showed business optimism climbing to a five-year high. Even so, Japanese government bonds were yielding only 2¾ percent. Our client, based on our recession call, decided to bet that those yields would fall much further. As the recession deepened, those yields approached 1 percent. Because the price of bonds rises when their yields drop, they profited handsomely from that recession call.

In June 1998, we made a presentation to the Bank of England at the behest of one of the monetary policy committee members, who was also an ECRI client. As luck would have it, the Bank had just raised interest rates that morning.

Awkwardly, our presentation showed a sharp weakening in the U.K. Long Leading Index of the economy, predicting a serious slowdown ahead, contrary to the convictions of the audience. Our host diplomatically concluded the meeting by saying that "the proof is in the pudding." Four months later, the Bank started slashing interest rates and the U.K. economy averted a recession.

As the late-1990s boom became an unsustainable bubble, many relied on their faith in a new paradigm to deny that a day of reckoning was at hand. The ECRI cube, on the other hand, detected the rise in inflation pressures that led the Fed to raise rates. This set the stage for a slowdown in economic activity, and the plunging profits and rising unemployment that would help trigger the 2001 recession. Moore did not live to see that call. A year to the day after his passing, our indicators plunged to such an extent that we were forced to make the recession call.

Many thought that Moore's personal experience and expertise had been responsible for the successful calls we had made in the past. When we predicted the recession of 1990–91, for instance, some chalked our success up to Moore's gut feel for the economy rather than credit the tools he had developed. The 2001 call proved once and for all that it was ECRI's indicators, viewed in the context of the cube, that made recessions and recoveries predictable. The success of the tools he developed is a fitting tribute to Moore's legacy.

When most analysts woke up to the reality of the recession, it was about to end. Our leading indicators of overall growth correctly called the recovery, but in early 2002, belated pessimism fueled much talk of a double-dip recession, which never happened. Then, as corporate scandals grew, geopolitical tensions flared up, and stock prices plunged, deflation fears became widespread. Our leading inflation indicators properly allayed those concerns as well.

In early 2003, economic growth was held back by the uncertainty surrounding the Iraq War. Once the war began and stocks rebounded, many expected job growth to snap right back, but our indicators told a different story. While the leading indexes of overall growth, along with the leading services index, pointed to a robust upturn, the leading manufacturing index languished, as did our leading employment index. The array of indicators that make up the cube correctly foresaw a lopsided recovery—more in GDP and less in jobs, more in services and less in manufacturing—pointing to a structural shift in manufacturing employment. Once again, our state-of-the-art forecasting tools cut through the confusion with clarity and precision.

THE ECONOMIC DASHBOARD

We have talked throughout this book about how you can use our work in economic cycle prediction to independently assess the course of the economy. The cube is the advanced version of an economic dashboard, a veritable jetliner cockpit of gauges and dials.

Few organizations or individuals need to view all of those dials in order to make better and more sophisticated economic decisions. In the next chapter, we will zero in on two key gauges from the cube to assemble a simple yet effective dashboard that will offer you an unbiased framework for monitoring and interpreting the course of the economy on your own.

PART THREE

The Economic
Dashbord

How to Read the Economic Indicators

When is it critical to know whether or not the economy is at a turning point? Whenever you are making a major decision and your success can be affected by a change in the economy. Major managerial decisions can range from expanding capacity, adding or closing down product lines or raising prices, to reallocating assets. Likewise, in your personal life, changes in the economy may influence key decisions such as buying a home or a car, making an investment, retiring, building a new addition to your home, deciding whether to switch jobs, or choosing whether to return to school for further study or an advanced degree.

Separately, you need to know when a leading index of the economy starts reversing direction in a *pronounced, pervasive,* and *persistent* manner—for it may be signaling a coming economic turn. If so, you should step back and consider how a major turn in the economic cycle would affect your interests.

By using our warning signals, you'll be able to adjust course to protect yourself, reduce risk, and perhaps take advantage of an emerging opportunity.

Sound too good to be true?

SOUR GRAPES SKEPTICISM

There are plenty of times in the course of a business cycle when you can relax and enjoy the ride. But there are also times when you need to pay more attention to the road ahead. The key is being able to forecast turning points in a timely and reliable fashion. Most economic pundits would say this is impossible—and their record bears them out.

The widespread failure of economists to predict recessions is due to the inadequacy of models rather than the inherent unpredictability of the economy. Nonetheless, there is broad skepticism that anyone can reliably predict turning points.

When we predicted the last two U.S. recessions, the initial reaction was disbelief. When we were proved right, most attributed it to luck.

This may be due to attribution bias, where people blame their own mistakes on circumstances beyond their control, and chalk up the successes of others to luck. Such skepticism can be dangerous to the extent that it keeps you from using the tools described in this book. To appreciate why they work, it is important to understand the sort of data that most analysts use to develop their views of the economy.

SO MUCH TO WATCH

The deluge of data and opinion on the economy is overwhelming. One popular data provider maintains four *million* economic variables. But 99.99 percent of them are useless for predicting cyclical turns. Worse, they are often misleading. Less than 0.01 percent of the information out there—that is, about 400 variables—is actually useful.

Every so often, an article about some expert's favorite list of economic indicators is published in the popular business magazines to help people assess the economy's prospects. But such indicators simply aren't reliable. First, a handful of indicators are not enough to give you a reliable compass setting on the economy's direction. Second, most of the indicators these pundits rely on inevitably come from the 99.99 percent that are useless. Finally, even if the indicators are useful, they often give contradictory signals, making it impossible to decipher what they mean.

Recently, a "secret" list of such indicators, provided by a former economic adviser to the President of the United States, was published in *Inc.* magazine.[1] Let's take a quick look at that list of indicators, and how they performed before and after the 2001 recession and recovery.

As you can see from the adjoining set of charts, one of these indicators, Retail Chain Store Sales, kept rising throughout the recession and recovery, seeming to suggest that the economy was getting stronger at the very time it was in full retreat. Another indicator, Commercial and Industrial Loans, peaked just before the recession began, providing little warning beforehand as to where the economy was headed. It also kept plunging long after the

Misleading Indicators?

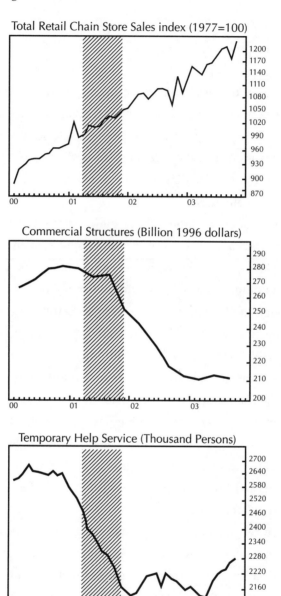

Total Retail Chain Store Sales index (1977=100)

Commercial Structures (Billion 1996 dollars)

Temporary Help Service (Thousand Persons)

Shaded areas represent business cycle recessions.

These "secret" indicators from a top economist are supposed to provide early warning of changes in the economy, yet two of them

Commercial and Industrial Loans (Billion Dollars)

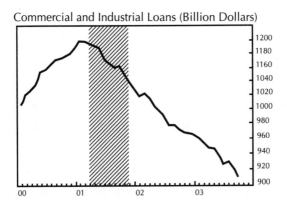

North American Semiconductor Book-to-Bill Ratio

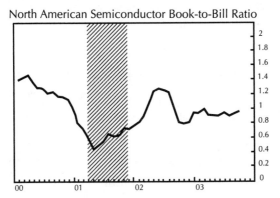

Part-Time Workers (Thousand Persons)

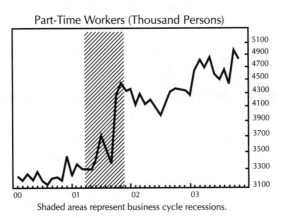

Shaded areas represent business cycle recessions.

completely miss the 2001 recession (shaded bar), three of them miss the recovery, and most of the time they contradict one another.

recovery had begun. A third indicator, Commercial Structures, similarly gave little warning of the impending downturn yet kept falling more than a year into the recovery. The Semiconductor Equipment Book-to-Bill Ratio actually did turn down before the recession began and turned up before the recovery, but that is only to be expected around a recession that was triggered in part by the implosion in the information technology sector. Another indicator, Temporary Help Service, gave early warning of the recession, but it did not bottom out until more than a year into the upturn, probably reflecting the jobless recovery. Finally, the Number of Part-Time Workers actually started *rising* before the recession, and kept climbing through the recession and recovery. Our point is that these indicators were both misleading and contradictory during the latest cycle. How is one to interpret them? Yet they were put forth as the key indicators used by the nation's top economists.

Nor is this confusion confined to the United States. In October of 2000, ECRI attended a conference in Europe to present our outlook for Germany. Based on our German Long Leading Index, which had been plunging, we predicted an economic downturn. The consensus among German economists was for strong growth in 2001. In fact, the expectation was that German growth would soon outpace that of the United States. As it turned out, Germany went into recession in January 2001, two months before the United States did.

After our presentation, several attendees expressed strong disagreement with our pessimistic outlook, including the chief economist of a major German car company. "You're wrong," he told us flatly. His favorite indicators showed just the opposite. Emphasizing the thoroughness of his analysis, he explained that one of his assistants updated those special indicators daily, and that the economic outlook was quite rosy. His clinching argument was that all the best German economists, whom he knew personally, agreed that a downturn was impossible. His company, to the extent they calibrated their business to the expectation of a growing economy, experienced a nasty surprise.

These examples illustrate the danger of relying too casually on someone else's set of pet indicators, even if they have worked well in the past. So what is our secret? What are the components of the leading indexes we have created, and why do they work when others fail? Unfortunately, there is no short list of indicators that will work for every circumstance. And no single indicator has proven to be the Holy Grail of economic forecasting. Instead, we regularly monitor hundreds of indicators that have proven their worth over time. We have found that different indicators take turns at being accurate predictors. Trying to anticipate which one is going to accurately forecast the next turn in the economy is a fool's errand.

But, over time, we have identified a limited number of drivers of the economic cycle that, taken together, can show where the economy is headed. While it is impossible for us to know which individual *driver* will take the lead at the next turning point, *together* they can detect early signs of an upcoming turn in the economy with near certainty.

Keep in mind that even among the drivers—such as profits, inventories, and the money supply—there can be disagreement about where things are headed. We resolve this ambiguity by determining good proxy measures for the various drivers—that is, individual leading indicators—and combining them into composite indexes, which objectively summarize their information. For example, in constructing the Weekly Leading Index (WLI), we use a specific leading indicator—initial claims for unemployment insurance—to represent employment, which is a key driver of the business cycle. Likewise, we pick out six other specific leading indicators that are updated weekly, to represent other cyclical forces. Because the seven indicators are rarely unanimous, we summarize them into the composite WLI, which distills the information into a single summary predictor of the economy's direction.

To accurately assess cyclical risk, two aspects of the economy must be monitored: economic growth and inflation. Together they largely determine what most individuals and smaller businesses need to know to navigate the ups and downs in the economy. (Larger corporations, as we discuss later, may need more detailed information.)

THE WEEKLY LEADING INDEX AND FUTURE INFLATION GAUGE

We have developed two composite leading indexes for U.S. growth and inflation that we have made publicly available in business magazines, financial newswires, and on our website (businesscycle.com). The Weekly Leading Index (WLI) anticipates cycles in overall economic activity—recessions and recoveries—by summarizing the best leading indicators of growth at a given time. This allows one to focus on a single measure to get a read on the overall business cycle outlook. The other index, the Future Inflation Gauge (FIG), summarizes the best leading indicators of inflation. This is important because inflationary pressures influence changes in interest rates.

Think of these two indexes as the temperature and fuel

gauges on your economic dashboard. You don't need to be a car mechanic to be able to read the fuel level and engine temperature of your car. Similarly, monthly glances at the FIG will allow you to assess how hot the economy is running. The Weekly Leading Index will tell you if the economy is ready to race forward or about to run out of gas.

You should check the WLI and the FIG regularly—at least once a month. Missing a week won't mean the end of the world, but we strongly recommend that you never let extended periods of time pass without knowing what the indicators are saying.

On the cusp of a major business or life decision, you will need to watch the signals more closely. You should also know what steps to take when a warning light suddenly goes on, signaling a turn in growth or inflation. When a clear change in direction is indicated in either the WLI or the FIG, you need to pay closer attention and plan for the possibility of an imminent shift in the economy.

In watching the dashboard, you are actually looking for upcoming turning points. By a turning point in economic activity, we mean a shift from economic expansion to contraction, or vice versa. A turning point in inflation is a shift from falling to rising inflation, or vice versa. When you approach a turning point, the risk of believing the consensus view balloons dramatically. Most people's perceptions of risk lag reality; a turning point represents the key moment when following the pack will lead you dangerously astray. If the WLI or FIG plunges or rises in a convincing manner, it is signaling an imminent turning point in its cycle.

Just what do we mean when we say "in a convincing manner"? As we explained in the last chapter, in order to be considered a true cyclical turn, the movement must be *pronounced*, *pervasive*, and *persistent*.

Economic Dashboard

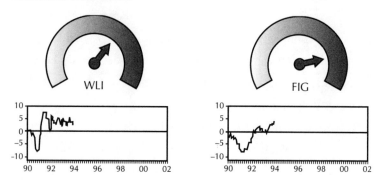

The basic dashboard consists of the WLI and the FIG. If the WLI is weak, the economy is in danger of stalling out. If the FIG is too strong, it's in danger of overheating.

- How Pronounced? The movement in the index needs to be comparable in magnitude to past cyclical swings. We suggest looking at cyclical swings during the recessions of 1990–91 and 2001, or the recoveries that followed, to give yourself a good idea of what a pronounced swing looks like (see chart on the next page).
- How Pervasive? The movement has to be driven not by one or two indicators, but by a majority of the index's components. In addition to our website, you can find free articles on the indexes through Reuters, Bloomberg, and Dow Jones that will give you this information.
- How Persistent? The movement cannot be just a temporary spike, but must be a change in direction that lasts at least three or four months.

At private presentations of our outlook, we are often asked basic questions about how to read ECRI's indexes.

Weekly Leading Index, Growth Rate (%)

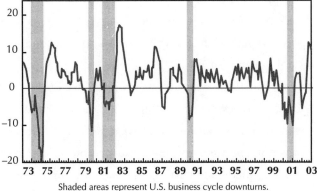

Shaded areas represent U.S. business cycle downturns.

When a pervasive weakness in its components causes WLI growth to fall well below zero, it is predicting a recession. A rebound back above zero signals a recovery.

One common question is: How can I tell that the Weekly Leading Index (WLI) leads the economy's turning points?

A: Look at the graph above. The shaded areas in the graph mark the recession periods, while the white areas represent periods of economic expansion. Major declines in Weekly Leading Index growth below zero lead the onset of recessions, just as the rebound back above zero from those declines anticipate recoveries. This means that when the level of the WLI falls substantially, its growth rate will drop well below zero, pointing to an upcoming recession. Thus, it is the *level* of the Weekly Leading Index that indicates cyclical downswings before recessions and upswings before recoveries. In fact, cyclical upturns and downturns in the index are designed to anticipate the turns in the *business cycle*, while upturns and downturns in the *growth rate* of the index anticipate turns in the *growth rate cycle*.

Another common question is: How come in 1983 the chart shows a big plunge, but no recession followed?

A: Notice that WLI growth did not fall as far below zero as it had in previous recessions. In other words, the decline in the WLI was not *pronounced*.

What about in 1987, when WLI growth fell well below zero?

A: Growth in the Weekly Leading Index did fall below zero, but it was pulled down almost single-handedly by stock prices. Thus, it was not a *pervasive* decline. Information on how pervasively the components are turning is available from free news stories on the Internet every Friday.

What about the drop in 1998? Why did that not trigger a recession?

A: That was a close call. The drop in the WLI was somewhat pronounced and pervasive, but it was reversed very quickly. As a result, it failed to be a *persistent* enough decline to forecast recession.

What did the Weekly Leading Index predict when it fell in 2002?

A: Its decline was not pronounced, pervasive, and persistent enough to forecast a new recession. However, it was correct in anticipating the downturn in growth, meaning the economy continued to expand, but more slowly. The WLI also anticipated similar slowdowns in 1984, 1987, 1994, and 1998.

What exactly is the Future Inflation Gauge designed to do?

A: The FIG is a measure of underlying inflationary pressures. It anticipates cyclical peaks and troughs in inflation, as defined by the growth rate of the Consumer Price Index. The FIG is a particularly useful index for investors and finance managers, since the inflation rate impacts interest rates including the Federal Funds Rate, as well as stock and bond prices. You can see from the chart

U.S. Future Inflation Gauge

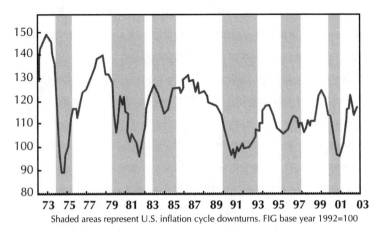

Shaded areas represent U.S. inflation cycle downturns. FIG base year 1992=100

*Cyclical upswings in the FIG anticipate rising inflation, while a
downswing in the FIG foretells periods of falling inflation.*

above that the Future Inflation Gauge turns down before the
shaded areas representing inflation downswings, and turns up
before the white areas, which mark off the upswings in inflation.

Inflation was basically low and stable in the 1990s. So why
did the FIG move up and down so much?

A: While it is true that inflation was relatively low, there were
clear cyclical swings in inflation during the 1990s. More important, there were large preemptive swings in the Federal Funds
Rate, which in effect reduced the size of the swings in inflation.
For example, the Fed raised interest rates aggressively in
1994–95, but Consumer Price Index inflation still rose from 2.3
percent in May 1994 to 3.2 percent a year later. Again, the Fed
tried to curb inflation by raising rates sharply in 1999–2000;
nevertheless, CPI inflation climbed from 1.4 percent in the
spring of 1998 to 3.8 percent two years later, and did not subside

until 2001 in the wake of the recession. Inflation then rose from just 1.1 percent in June 2002 to 3 percent by February 2003. The Future Inflation Guage foretold each of these upturns in inflation, as well as the downturns that followed.

Even with a better idea about how to interpret the Weekly Leading Index and the Future Inflation Gauge, it is not realistic to expect that you will be warned of a turning point six months in advance each and every time. The lead times can vary. Sometimes the warning of an economic turning point becomes apparent even earlier. At other times, there is no warning until much later. As Geoffrey H. Moore once reminded us, if you can "predict" a recession just as it is beginning, you are doing very well as a forecaster. This is because most people are unaware of recessions until they are almost over. The 2001 recession was no exception. The recession began in March of 2001. Nonetheless, the stock market rallied that spring despite the fact that a recessionary bear market was under way. The recession's start date wasn't officially recognized until November 2001—the very month it ended. Whether you predict a recession months in advance or recognize one as it begins, you will always be far ahead of the pack.

Average Lead of Weekly Leading Index (WLI)
and Future Inflation Gauge (FIG)

	Lead at Troughs (months)	Lead at Peaks (months)
WLI, against business cycle turning points	3	10
FIG, against inflation cycle turning points	9	12

The Future Inflation Gauge's leads at peaks and troughs in inflation are fairly similar. The WLI's lead at upturns in the economy is generally *shorter* than the lead at *downturns* (see table on facing page). Even in predicting upturns, however, the index provides significant warning as compared with the general perception of the marketplace. The WLI can give one conviction and certainty about the economy's direction even as others remain confused.

TALES FROM THE TRENCHES

Many Fortune 500 companies use ECRI's leading indexes to help guide their actions. But you are unlikely to hear them talk openly about this. Because they operate in a cutthroat environment, they are loath to highlight the sources of their competitive advantages. Nonetheless, a few of ECRI's clients are willing to share with you their experiences in using our cyclical outlook to help guide their decisions.

The Martin Tractor Company, a distributor of Caterpillar products located in Topeka, Kansas, is one such client. Martin Tractor is a fourth-generation family-owned company employing 280 people. Harry Craig, the chairman and CEO, is also an ordained minister. According to Mr. Craig, ECRI's forecasts help them remain true to the company's core values of "responsible stewardship"—a "financially sound" operation that can "provide security, stability and profit sharing" for their employees and customers.

Martin Tractor's fiscal year ends in June. At their August 2002 board meeting, the CFO reported that the fiscal year just ended was the third best in company history. The sales manager said,

"Overall, I continue to be optimistic." The president and COO reported, "Compared to last year's first half, this year looks like a barnburner." However, alluding to ECRI's indexes, he noted, "There are some trends that need to be watched." That month ECRI had concluded that the construction sector would weaken (see chart below). Sure enough, as Mr. Craig would later recall, "For many of us in the heavy equipment industry, the second six months of 2002 was a disaster."

ECRI's third-quarter reports significantly influenced the amount of inventory ordered by Martin Tractor. While their gut told them that the second half of 2002 would be at least as good as the first, ECRI's reports suggested that the construction sector was heading south. "Because of ECRI our inventories were in far

U.S. Leading Construction Index, Growth Rate (%) January 1999–July 2002

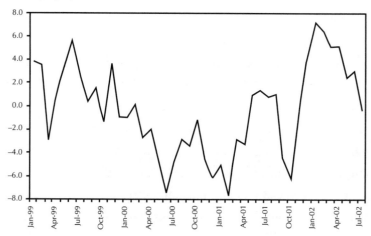

The drop in this index through the summer of 2002 warned Martin Tractor that the construction sector was heading south.

better shape at the end of 2002 than they would have been if we had listened to our 'gut,'" Mr. Craig says.

Three months later, in November 2002, when Martin Tractor was ordering up inventory for 2003, ECRI reported that prospects for the construction sector had dimmed (see chart below). The report confirmed Martin Tractor's own instincts. As a result, by mid-2003, they were "right-sized" regarding inventory for the year.

A cyclical worldview can be an enormous benefit to even our larger clients—from Toyota Motors to the Taiwan Semiconductor Manufacturing Company. For cyclical businesses in particular, like those in most manufacturing industries and those that depend on discretionary expenditures, management decisions

U.S. Leading Construction Index, Growth Rate (%) January 1999–October 2002

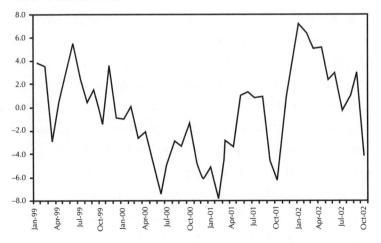

By the fall of 2002, this index had plunged even further, affirming the bleak near-term outlook for construction.

about production and pricing can have a dramatic impact on profitability. DuPont, a leading chemical company made up of many businesses that compete worldwide, is a prominent example. DuPont has been a client of ECRI's for many years. They monitor a broad array of our leading indexes, from sector-specific information to global indexes. In the late 1990s, one division had become particularly skilled at using this information in making business decisions.

In the fall of 1998, in the wake of the Russian default and the LTCM debacle, President Clinton warned the country of what he thought was the worst financial crisis in fifty years. The Fed, in response, made three emergency rate cuts. Recession fears became widespread. But while apprehensive competitors were cutting prices, the DuPont division in question held its ground because the ECRI leading indexes it monitored did not show a downturn ahead. As a result, it was able to handily outperform its competitors.

In late 1999, with the boom back on track, complacency had once again set in. However, the leading indexes that related to their business were pointing to a cyclical downturn in late 2000. Knowing that, the division managers took preemptive steps, aggressively pushing sales and reducing inventories in the first half, in anticipation of a lean second half. When industry demand began to slump in the second half of 2000, they were well positioned, having already pared down inventories. These experiences became the stuff of legend within DuPont.

Our money manager clients have also benefited from advance warning of turns in the cycle. In 1995, following the worst year in the bond market's history, there were widespread apprehensions that the slowdown in the economy would evolve into a recession. In fact, some prominent Wall Street firms forecast just that. ECRI's leading indexes, however, pointed to continued expansion. We were able to reassure our client, a West Coast mutual fund, that the risk of a recessionary bear market was low. Accordingly, they were aggressively long in the stock market. As we now know, 1995 marked the beginning of the Great Bull Market of the late 1990s.

We mentioned another client in Chapter 7, one of the nation's largest mutual funds, who took the 1996 plunge in ECRI's Japanese Long Leading Index very seriously, even though it went against the prevailing consensus of market participants. If we were correct, Japanese stocks were not the place to be investing at that time. Based on our findings, our client purchased substantial quantities of Japanese government bonds instead, at a yield of just $2\frac{3}{4}$ percent. As the recession took hold, those yields plunged by almost two-thirds. Because the price of bonds rises when their yields drop, they were able to book a large profit on that trade, rather than experience a significant loss in equities.

In late 1999, an investment manager and longtime ECRI client noted a seismic shift in market risks. For years he had read our analysis attributing inflation-free growth of the 1990s to the fact that different national economies took turns going into recession, keeping global overcapacity intact. When we predicted a Japanese recovery in 1999, resulting in a synchronous global expansion, he realized that inflation pressures would soon build. The persistent rise in the Future Inflation Gauge gave him the confirmation he needed. While other managers assumed that the Federal Reserve's rate hikes would be limited to taking back the three emergency rate cuts made in the wake of the 1998 LTCM crisis, he anticipated that the Fed was just getting started.

He first reduced his exposure to bonds; then he began cutting back on his asset allocation to stocks, in the belief that the Fed action would cause a cyclical downturn in growth, driving stock prices down. As it turned out, he was a few months early in anticipating the stock market top, and took some heat for underperforming during the last days of the bull market. But he was well positioned for the vicious bear market that followed.

When we warned of recession in September 2000, a New York–based hedge fund client used his confidence in our cyclical forecast to bet that the Fed Funds Rate would fall much more than was currently priced into the market. It is worth remembering that even though the FIG had been falling since April 2000, Fed statements through November maintained that the risk of higher inflation was greater than that of economic weakness. A few weeks later, in January 2001, the Fed began a historic series of rate cuts that would bring the Funds Rate down to a forty-five-year low. Consequently, the fund's returns were astronomical.

MANAGING RISK ON THE JOB

Most individuals and small-business owners can use the Weekly Leading Index and the Future Inflation Gauge to help time major decisions and alert them to turns in growth and inflation. However, if you are responsible for decisions guiding a large institution, there are additional tools you should be using. As a corporate executive responsible for planning, an investment manager responsible for other people's money, or a policy maker responsible for guiding a national economy, you'll need a more extensive dashboard with a whole array of leading indexes—the kind of economic cycle cube we discussed in Chapter 7. In order to make a more sophisticated decision, it may be important to know whether the service sector will grow while manufacturing weakens, whether a recovery will be a jobless one, if strength in construction will evaporate soon, whether credit availability is likely to worsen, or if German export growth will soon improve. Because such detailed insights are often vital for these decision makers, we have created *more than a hundred* indexes to monitor the many cycles that make up the global economy. Most of our indexes are extremely focused and help industry professionals manage risk, corporate executives to plan, and money managers to make asset-allocation decisions. Our work with these clients helps us finance our ongoing research. At the same time, the WLI and the FIG are widely available to everyone who needs help navigating the business cycle.

USING THE INDEXES IN YOUR PERSONAL LIFE

Michael Drury is an entrepreneur in New York City. In the early 1990s, when he was still in college, he actively day-traded stock index options. That was about the time he started following our leading indexes through financial news stories.

By the mid-1990s, he had opened a bar in downtown Manhattan, taking advantage of a weak real estate market to negotiate a favorable lease. While he retained a majority stake, some of the start-up capital came from private investors. Business soon took off, and as the city's economy benefited from the late-1990s boom, his profits swelled. The time was ripe to expand operations, and he opened a second bar that included a restaurant. All the while, Michael had kept an eye on the climbing Weekly Leading Index, which continued to predict a growing economy.

By the fall of 2000, the WLI was in a clear decline, but business remained brisk. Still, Michael made a deliberate effort to pay particular attention to the WLI updates every Friday. By early 2001, he became genuinely concerned about the WLI's continued slide; as a result, despite soaring profits, he decided not to increase payouts to his investors. With the stock market rallying that spring, this decision did not sit well with them. But with ECRI now publicly predicting a recession, he was willing to take the heat.

Michael knew that the summer months were usually weak for his business because many residents left town. He and his competitors had always seen a rebound in business when people returned in the fall. But he had never seen the Weekly Leading Index plunge this way before. He decided not to count on the usual bounce in revenue. This meant putting off expanding the business, postponing capital outlays that he had earlier planned; he actually reduced payouts to his investors. As a result, the business began accumulating cash, which would place it in a more stable position if the WLI was right about a recession.

The rally in equities petered out in late spring. All summer and into early September 2001, stocks continued to slide as the reality of the recession sank in. Then came the events of September 11. Michael's bar, along with scores of other businesses, temporarily closed. In the aftermath, downtown Manhattan was paralyzed. Still, Michael decided to reopen the week after the tragedy, even though it was clear that there would be no revival in business anytime soon.

The WLI bottomed in October 2001, just before the U.S. recession ended. Downtown Manhattan took much longer to recover, and many bars and restaurants went out of business. Thanks to Michael's foresight, his business had the staying power to keep going through those dark days.

Not everyone has a small business to run. But understanding the business cycle can help individuals make all kinds of decisions.

Rena Rosen (not her real name) is a retiree living on fixed-income investments. In January 1994, she had most of her money in long-term Treasury bonds and long-term bond mutual funds, because she needed the higher yields to live on. With several of her T-bonds maturing, she had to decide whether to roll them over into new long-term bonds or, given the low yields in early 1994, wait for those yields to climb.

While not an economist, Rena was interested in economics and current affairs. She had heard of our work from her son, who had been a graduate student at Columbia University when our research group was housed there. She understood that when inflation pressures rise, interest rates follow. She also learned that the FIG was an excellent gauge to measure underlying inflationary pressures.

By January 1994, her dashboard showed her that the FIG had turned up. The risk of a rise in interest rates was clear to her (see upper panel of the "Economic Dashboard" on the next page). In order to protect her savings, she would need to move her money into short-term T-bills and money market funds. Unfortunately, this would not give her much of an income. She was understandably reluctant to make such a bold move, especially since nobody else was raising an alarm. So she called us—not to ask for invest-

Economic Dashboard

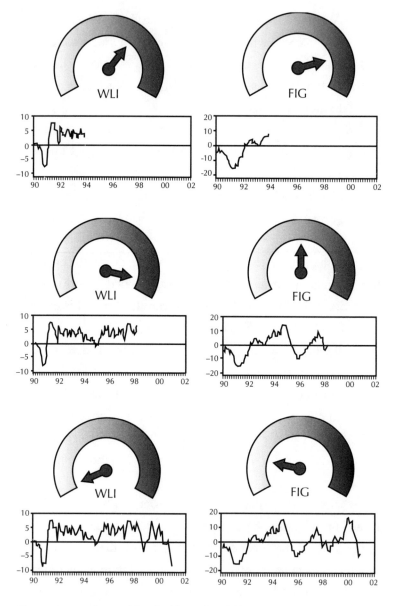

*Here are snapshots of the dashboard at different points in time.
The upper panel shows the situation in early 1994, the middle panel
shows it at the end of 1998, and the lower panel in early 2001.*

ment advice, but simply to check if we really believed that the FIG was a good gauge of inflation pressures. We assured her that it was the best measure we knew of. As a result, she went ahead and sold her bond funds, putting the money from her matured T-bonds into short-term T-bills that would not lose as much value if interest rates rose.

Nineteen-ninety-four turned out to be the worst year in the bond market's sixty-year history, and long-term bonds plunged in value. A great deal of investment capital was lost. Rena had dodged a bullet, thanks to her reading of the FIG. Once it peaked and turned down in 1995, she again bought shares in her old bond mutual fund, which were now much cheaper. She claims that our inflation forecast spelled the difference between a "comfortable retirement" and a situation she would rather not think about.

In the early fall of 1998, a financial crisis was sparked by Russia's debt default, and many feared that a recession was at hand. Prices of high-yield (or "junk") bonds plunged in the expectation of more business failures. But Treasury bond yields plummeted, reflecting a flight to quality, and Rena's bond mutual fund gained solidly in value.

Meanwhile, ECRI's leading indicators of economic activity were already rising, assuring her that there was no recession ahead (see middle panel of chart). So she sold her shares in the long-term bond fund at a good profit and bought shares in a high-yield bond fund. When recession fears abated in 1999, the value of those shares soared, leaving her with solid capital gains.

Two years later, in early 2001, the WLI plunged (see lower panel of chart) in anticipation of a recession, which would clearly damage her junk bonds as weak companies defaulted or went bankrupt. So she sold off those funds and bought Treasury bonds, which appreciated solidly in value over the next two years. A decade after her first decision based on ECRI's leading indexes, not only did she have much more money than she would have had otherwise, but she had navigated the market gyrations with far more peace of mind.

We advise *everyone* to watch the WLI and the FIG, but there are other ECRI indexes that some people will find helpful to monitor before making important decisions, such as a home purchase or sale. In this case, the Leading Home Price Index may be useful, as the following story illustrates.

Debbie Flanagan (not her real name) had purchased an apartment with her parents' help in 1990 when prices were relatively low. As a young professional, she paid close attention to economic experts on television. When the recession became evident in 2001, many of them predicted an imminent drop in home prices, in line with the experience in earlier recessions. On that basis, she and a friend both decided to sell their apartments immediately, and rent until prices had fallen substantially. They figured that they would be able to make some decent money by selling high and buying low.

As luck would have it, soon after she made that decision, she heard us mention our Leading Home Price Index on a financial television program. Unusually, the index was holding up in the face of the recession, and saw no decline in home prices ahead. Debbie rang up ECRI straightaway, and after confirming what she had heard, began to rethink her strategy. While she started dragging her feet on selling, her friend went full steam ahead and closed on the sale of her apartment. Months went by, but home prices kept rising. Debbie checked with ECRI again and, with the index now rising strongly, took her apartment off the market. Meanwhile, her friend was getting anxious about buying a new apartment, but prices were now almost 10 percent higher.

TAMING RISK

Michael and Rena ended up with much more money because they judiciously used the WLI and FIG to help in their decision making—and thanks to a bit of luck. Debbie used the Leading Home Price Index to make an informed decision about whether or not it was the right time to sell. In fact, these leading indexes are designed not to time the markets but to forecast turning points in growth, inflation in general, and home prices in particular. As a result, they are good for reducing the risks associated with economic shifts that often affect businesses and the financial and housing markets. Advance notice of risk allowed our clients to take precautionary measures when risks rose, and participate fully in lower-risk opportunities.

Like Michael and Rena, you too can execute your business and investment plans without being whipsawed by cyclical turns in growth and inflation. Rena, wanting to stay invested in bonds, simply used the cyclical outlook to help her decide when to move between long- and short-term Treasuries, and between Treasuries and lower-quality debt. Michael used the cycle forecasts to decide when to be cautious about expenses and expansion plans.

When growth is about to turn down, stocks get riskier and bonds become safer, especially if inflationary pressures are also falling. The converse is also true. Prior to an upturn in the economy, stocks become less risky, and once growth starts picking up bonds are more risky, especially if inflationary pressures are also on the rise (see chart below). Our indexes are designed to inform you of the outlook for growth and inflation.

The job market, too, is sensitive to economic growth, particularly in cyclical industries. If your dashboard warns of a downturn ahead and you are looking for a job, you may want to consider an industry less exposed to the ups and downs of the economy, like health care. If that is not an option, you should try to position yourself so that you are less likely to be laid off if your company or industry is forced to "cut costs."

Cyclical Patterns in Stock and Bond Prices

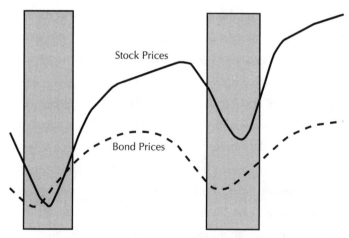

Shaded areas represent business cycle recessions.

This is a stylized illustration of the behavior of stock and bond prices over the course of the business cycle.

In the next chapter, we examine some scenarios showing how our indexes can help you make better choices. These scenarios are pretty good models to help you recognize shifting risks and what signs to look for when making—or putting off—decisions. In real life, events may not play out as precisely as we outline. The financial markets, for example, can on occasion confound any observer. But the settings we describe clearly demonstrate how you can reduce the risk of an unpleasant outcome.

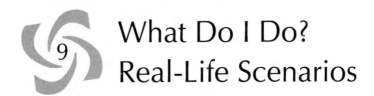

What Do I Do?
Real-Life Scenarios

A: PERSONAL AFFAIRS

Nest Egg

Let's say that you have just retired with a nest egg of $400,000. You're healthy, plan to live a long life, and would also like to travel around the world and help your grandkids pay for college. In order to do all of these things, you will need a better return on your money than government bonds will provide, so you're thinking about putting a significant part of your savings in stocks.

You see that the Future Inflation Gauge (FIG) is rising, while the Weekly Leading Index (WLI) growth is heading down— already WLI growth has dropped from 7 percent to 1 percent in four months. You know that a higher FIG suggests rising inflationary pressures, and a fall in WLI growth points to a downturn in economic growth, and possibly recession. Historically, the prospect of an economic downturn has been bad for stock prices, while bonds should become attractive once the FIG turns down. What should you do?

Based on these indications from the WLI and the FIG, you may need to reassess your portfolio's risk exposure. One option is to move most of your money into cash and watch closely for any change in the direction of either index. If the FIG falls by five to ten points, bonds would become far less risky. Later, when WLI growth turns up well above zero, it would be safer to get back into stocks. You are unlikely to catch the bottom in stock or bond prices this way, but you will be positioned to ride most of the upswing in the market—that is, until the indexes turn again. Leo Melamed, chairman emeritus of the Chicago Mercantile Exchange, once observed that it's always better to get a chunk of the middle than to try to be precise at calling tops and bottoms in any financial market.

Windfall

Let's say you're young, under forty, and you inherit $200,000. What should you do with it? You probably won't want to let it burn a hole in your pocket. Let's suppose growth in the WLI is drifting down from 6 percent to 4 percent, and the FIG is fairly stable. You do not have a lot of conviction about the economy's fundamental strength or the prospects for stable inflation. Hard as it may be, the best course of action may be to keep your money in cash (and avoid trips to Vegas!). Meanwhile, watch the WLI and the FIG for signs of a shift in the economy.

Sometime later, WLI growth starts to move up to almost 10

percent, and more important, rises steadily over a few months. Meanwhile, the level of the FIG also starts a more gentle rise, climbing from 106 to 109 in three months.

The wisest decision in this case could be to place most of your money in growth stocks, as the risk of a stock bear market has receded dramatically.

Job or School?

Suppose you are a graduating senior in college. You are excited about the various options that lie in front of you. Last year's graduates by and large all found good jobs, and this year your classmates think things will be even better.

But your mom, who once shared your enthusiasm, and was helping you research firms in your field, suddenly urges you to apply for graduate studies, which you were planning to do after a few years on the job. Apparently, over the past year your mom has seen the WLI drop in a recessionary fashion—its growth rate has plunged from 8 percent to –9 percent—and she is convinced that the job market is turning sour. Furthermore, she thinks that once your classmates realize jobs are scarce, they will also apply to grad school en masse.

Should you follow her advice?

By all means. With the WLI dropping, the competition for school admission is hard, but nothing like what it will be next semester when we're deep in a downturn. Later on, if the WLI signals a strong recovery by rising well above zero, you may decide to accelerate your studies, earn your graduate degree a semester ahead of your classmates, and land a job before they are in a position to compete with you.

A Vulnerable Job

What if you are an IT professional in midcareer working for a large industrial corporation in the Northeast? You are alarmed to see the WLI growth rate plunging, and now the FIG is starting to decline as well. You've seen these patterns on the cusp of earlier recessions, so understandably you become concerned about job security, even though everyone at work remains unconcerned. What should you do?

Start looking for another job. Is there a way you can apply your expertise to a "recession-proof" industry like health care, education, or consumer staples? After all, computers are used in just about every industry. Doing so will place you at the front of the line for the ongoing hiring in these industries well before the deluge of applications that will appear once the recession takes hold.

New Business

Perhaps the company you work for is seeking to shrink its workforce in the wake of a recession, and you are tempted to accept the severance package being offered and use the money, along with a bank loan, to realize your dream of buying your own restaurant. As it happens, one of your favorite eateries—after losing money in the downturn—is up for sale at an affordable price.

But the WLI has been rising sharply, with its growth rate already at 11 percent, while the FIG is still falling. That suggests the economy will soon pick up, while interest rates will stay low for the time being. Should you quit your job and buy the restaurant?

If you've done your homework and are sure it's a good deal— after all, a poorly located restaurant is likely to be a bad investment regardless of the cyclical forecast—the time is certainly right to go ahead and fulfill your dream. The price will probably go up as business improves; if you wait until the economic recovery is obvious, the interest rates on the loan you need may no longer be that low. The indicators are telling you that it's the perfect time to make your move.

Spare Cash for Investing

Imagine you are a midcareer professional who just received a nice bonus, part of which you'd like to invest in the markets. Stock prices have started to rise after declining for several months, and you're wondering whether it's safe to buy some shares in an index mutual fund.

You notice that WLI growth has risen to 7.7 percent after an earlier decline to –0.5 percent, while the FIG is still falling. The WLI is pointing to a pickup in economic growth, but with inflationary pressures subdued, interest rates look unlikely to rise soon. It seems the recent rise in the markets is supported by the economic fundamentals captured by the indexes.

This is one of the safest scenarios for stock market investing. While you might have missed the bottom, the risk of a bear market is low under these circumstances.

Spare Cash to Spend

Maybe you and your husband have hit your peak earning years, and your children have finished college. You are thinking of dipping into your savings and splurging on an expensive vacation. You don't yet have enough savings to retire on, but if you keep saving this way until retirement, you should be fine. If you lose your job, though, you could be in trouble.

You notice that WLI growth has been falling lately, going

from 8 percent to −1 percent over the last six months, while the FIG is pretty flat. It is too early to predict a recession, but an economic slowdown could be in the cards. If the slowdown isn't too deep, you should be able to ride out the storm, but a deep downturn could jeopardize your job security. Should you take that dream vacation or wait?

Here's a case when it might be better to be prudent and postpone that vacation until the WLI sounds the all-clear signal. Hopefully, WLI growth will pick up soon rather than fall further. When the WLI starts to rise, an economic downturn becomes less probable, and you can feel more secure about spending some of your savings. You'll be less likely to lose your job—and more likely to enjoy your vacation!

Fiftieth Anniversary

What if you want to do something special to celebrate your golden wedding anniversary? You worked hard all your life, put your children through college, and, as you approach your eighties, you are not rich but have a comfortable life together. You have enough to live on for the rest of your lives, but still want to make sure you can leave a little money to your children. Most of your money is in bonds, but a sizable chunk is in stocks, which have done well in recent years.

But the celebration you are planning would put a dent in your total assets, and you worry that if the markets turn down sharply, you might end up leaving a smaller inheritance to your children than planned. What should you do?

Go ahead and celebrate—living life to the fullest during your golden years is much more important than any investment outlook.

B: CORPORATE DECISIONS

Pension Fund

Maybe like one of ECRI's clients, the manager of a large pension fund, you invest in both stocks and bonds in different portfolios. Because of a bull market in stocks, his equity funds have seen returns averaging 30 percent a year in the late 1990s.

Let's say you notice, as he did in the early spring of 2000, that the FIG is still rising but growth in the Long Leading Index (LLI) has turned down. Meanwhile, WLI growth is starting to slip, as are stock prices.

A slowdown—at the very least—lies ahead. You should follow his lead and prepare to lighten up on stocks, as well as plan to raise your allocation to bonds once the FIG starts falling. Soon after that, you would start to move back into stocks gradually, at first when LLI growth starts rising, and more aggressively when WLI growth starts climbing. As a result, you should outperform your peers, just as he did, having avoided most of the drops in stocks and bonds, and having taken advantage of most of their advances.

Hedge Fund

Suppose you manage a hedge fund, like some of ECRI's clients, and have wide discretion about how to invest the funds entrusted to you. After a long expansion, you see the Long Leading Index growth rate plunging, WLI growth flattening out, and the FIG starting to fall. These are the classic signs of an upcoming slowdown that is likely to hurt stocks once the reality sinks in. What should you do?

One clear course of action is to exit any long positions in stock futures, and instead establish long positions in Treasury bond futures, knowing that you would later exit bond futures and start buying stock futures and high-yield bonds when LLI growth turns up. You should be more aggressive about both strategies when WLI growth turns up.

As a result, you'd continue to handily beat the returns of most other hedge funds, particularly during periods of confusion about the economy's direction.

Major Domestic Industrial Corporation

As the CEO of a Fortune 500 company, you need to be especially sensitive to shifts in the economic environment. This is particularly true because you supply a wide range of industrial products to other companies rather than directly to the consumer. With the economy in an upturn, both your sales and profits have grown handsomely in recent years. But as the annual budget planning meeting for next year approaches, you wonder whether your sales team's optimistic projections are realistic.

While the WLI is still climbing, its growth rate has eased from 12 percent to 10 percent in recent months. In itself, that signals strong GDP growth. But because your concerns are more specific, you monitor ECRI's industry-specific indexes. You notice that the Leading Manufacturing Index (LMI) growth rate has dropped sharply from 21 percent to –8 percent, even though the leading indexes for services and construction have stayed strong. Growth in the Leading Manufacturing *Employment* Index is looking even worse.

In early 2003, ECRI warns of a structural shift in manufacturing jobs, although nobody else is talking about it. ECRI's analysis shows that the pattern of decline in manufacturing employment is dismal compared to the same stage of any past expansion. The implications are unsettling, because for your firm this may be a double whammy.

Think about it. Even though manufacturing activity will continue to expand, the decline in LMI growth suggests that your demand for your products will downshift, probably below your customer firms' projections. When that happens, just like the shoe manufacturers in Chapter 3, your customers will probably *cut* orders—so a general manufacturing *slowdown* could mean a *drop* in orders for your company.

But the structural change in manufacturing is an added threat, because it implies that your customers may outsource some of their production to Asia. This might imply a much larger plunge in your orders than a simple manufacturing slowdown. It could mean an entire restructuring of your business and laying off a significant portion of your workforce.

What should you do? First, you should lower your sales projections for next year and plan accordingly, cutting back on inventories and orders for raw materials. Second, you need to move aggressively to capture the business lost due to outsouring. You might even be forced to consider setting up your own factory in China to supply your customers' Asian factories.

Large Exporter

You are the chief operating officer of a large manufacturer of precision tools; exports account for more than half of your sales. As a major exporter competing mostly with German firms for business in Asia and Western Europe, you have taken a hit during the global recession. Furthermore, the strong U.S. dollar has been an added handicap because it has made your products more expensive to foreign buyers. As a result, your sales have slumped, and you've had to make painful cutbacks in personnel and close down a couple of plants. More cutbacks are planned, on the assumption that the tough times will continue. Your only consolation is that, thanks to ECRI's early warning about the first global recession in a generation, you had been very cautious since early 2001, and had persuaded your CEO not to build the new plant he had considered at the height of the boom.

But after examining your economic dashboard—which is far more sophisticated than the average investor's—you find that growth in the U.S. Leading Exports Index has turned up, rising to multiyear highs and pointing to much stronger export growth. In particular, ECRI's Asian long leading indexes have strengthened substantially, and the dollar has weakened against the euro, making your prices more attractive than your German competitors'. You are also intrigued that the Japanese Leading Manufacturing Index (JLMI) is starting to edge up. Is it finally time to try and tap the Japanese market?

Yes, it is. First, you should consider putting the planned cutbacks on hold. Once you see decisive upturns in the JLMI and ECRI's Manufacturing Related Diffusion Index of international manufacturing long leading indicators—which predicts the global industrial cycle—you should ramp up raw material orders in preparation for boosting production, focusing on what the international leading indexes suggest are the most promising markets. By making this timely move, you'll be in a position to grab market share from your less optimistic European competitors.

Cruise Line

Suppose you are the chief sales manager of a luxury cruise line whose business is highly dependent on discretionary consumer spending patterns. Business has been booming lately, along with the global economy. People in the industry are very optimistic, and your CEO is wondering how to speed up delivery of a new cruise liner you've ordered.

But you notice that growth in ECRI's U.S. Services Leading Index has started to drop, which suggests some easing in demand growth ahead. The weakness is also reflected in a slumping U.S. Long Leading Index and Weekly Leading Index, indicating that the overall economy will soon start to slow. Finally, ECRI's analysis shows that spiking oil prices will act like a tax on consumers, squeezing their cash flow. All of this is likely to hurt consumer discretionary expenditures—your bread and butter—even though business remains very good so far. How do you deal with the looming storm clouds?

There is hope. Keep in mind that the general optimism in the industry gives you a chance to sail to safety. First, you should see what you can do about stretching out the delivery time for that new ship. Next, you should move swiftly to offer attractive special deals, and sell advance bookings aggressively in order to get a jump on your competitors. By the time they realize that business is down, you'll be in relatively good shape and won't be forced to have a fire sale when consumers are unwilling to buy. You will also have increased your market share, which will benefit you when business picks up, especially if you receive the new ship soon after the leading indexes turn up—the very time when your competitors will likely be drowning in belated pessimism.

Advertising Agency

Say you are the CFO of a big ad agency, which has been thriving during the economic boom. Your business depends heavily on business spending, which is linked to the corporate profits that have been soaring. Your agency's profits have gone through the roof and, given strong sales projections, the firm is planning to hire more people and build a larger headquarters building. And as cash keeps rolling in, the board is considering raising the dividend.

You have agreed with these plans so far—until you notice that growth in the U.S. Long Leading Index has fallen sharply and growth in the Weekly Leading Index and Short Leading Index is also starting to ease. These are clear signs of a slowdown ahead—maybe even a recession. Should you push for a change in plans?

Under the circumstances, that would be wise. As you know, when growth slows, even if there is no recession, corporate profits always fall. Since corporate profits are a major driver of discretionary business spending—including advertising—your own sales could actually be headed for a downturn. Your earnings are likely to disappoint in a matter of months.

It may make sense to postpone the increase in dividends, cut back on hiring plans, and put off plans for a new headquarters building. If the indexes start to worsen in a recessionary fashion—for example, if growth in the Long Leading, Weekly Leading, and Short Leading Indexes falls well below zero—you could suggest that the firm chase after business in recession-resistant sectors like health care, insurance, political campaigns, consumer staples, and education. This way, your firm will still have cash and clients when the downturn hits.

Construction Company

As the CEO of a large construction company, you've seen your firm prosper during the economic upturn, with sales and profits hitting new records each quarter. But in early 2001 the economy is going into recession, just as ECRI's leading indexes predicted, and you know that housing has always suffered during recessions. In fact, everybody says that the housing bubble is about to burst. Should you prepare for that downturn and pull back on home construction?

You find that the Leading Construction Index (LCI) is weak, but the Leading Home Price Index (LHPI) remains strong. How should you react?

A weak LCI and strong LHPI indicate that while construction in general, and commercial business in particular, may be hit by the recession, home prices will remain robust for the time being. You could therefore plan to concentrate on the residential portion of your business.

Still, you know that home building is cyclical, so a downturn will eventually arrive. Take advantage of the housing boom as long as it lasts, while keeping an eye on the LHPI for signs of weakness. You might also begin to cultivate relationships in recession-resistant sectors like health care, education, defense, and homeland security, so that you will be ready to shift focus as soon as the LHPI starts to flag.

Deli Owner

You own a gourmet deli opposite the headquarters of one of the world's largest software producers. As that company has prospered and bonuses have grown, your business has flourished. In fact, in addition to expanding your existing facilities, you're considering opening another deli opposite a big business-software firm across town, and putting your excess cash in aggressive growth stocks—including those recommended by your customers.

But you notice that WLI growth, after a long rise, is falling sharply. What should you do?

Clearly, a growth rate downturn—and possibly a recession—is ahead. This is a risky time to be investing in stocks. Also, that business-software firm across town will probably lose business during such a downturn, so you should hold off on opening that new deli until after the recession, when the asking price and interest rates may be much lower. Wait until you see a pronounced, pervasive, and persistent upturn in WLI growth, which will also signal a safe entry point into stock purchases. Until then, you should hoard your cash instead of expanding your capacity—if business suffers during the downturn, that extra cash will come in handy.

Travel Agency

Suppose you manage a medium-sized travel agency that caters to several big businesses. Business has been very good during the boom, and you are already stretched to capacity. You are planning to hire at least one more assistant. You are also thinking of renovating the office to make it look more upscale than the other travel agency in the neighborhood.

Then you notice WLI growth turning down sharply. The FIG is also falling. You realize a slowdown in economic growth is ahead, one that will inevitably shave corporate profits. This is exactly the moment when such firms tend to cut back on discretionary expenditures like travel. What should you do?

Obviously, you should postpone hiring those assistants and spending money on renovations. Later on, once the downturn is about to end—which will be signaled by a pronounced upturn in WLI growth—you might consider taking out a low-interest loan to purchase your competitor. That's also the best time for renovations.

Having said this, you should understand that your industry is in the throes of a permanent structural change driven by the economics of Internet-based travel bookings. This structural shift will not be reversed when the WLI turns back up.

Perhaps none of these examples *exactly* resembles the choices you face today. But they should give you a good idea of the kinds of decisions that are critical during upturns, downturns—and in between. Obviously, many events—war and peace, natural disasters, and long-term structural shifts—can never be predicted by leading indexes. But if you make wise moves before the economy turns, you'll be much better prepared for whatever difficulty—or blessing—life throws your way.

All you have to do is trust the indexes. Of course, we already know this is the hardest part of adopting a cyclical worldview. That's why our final chapter will remind you how crucial it is to break from the pack before it's too late, and what to do when you start to doubt your dashboard.

10 The Discipline of a Cyclical Approach

Keeping an eye on your economic dashboard is easy. The hard part is trusting what it tells you, especially when that information goes against the grain of public opinion. When you adopt a cyclical worldview, your outlook will be in the minority whenever the chance of an economic turning point is high. We cannot stress enough how important it is to keep this in mind. After all, it is one thing to accept such a notion in theory, but quite another to have the confidence to act on it when your job, business, or personal assets are on the line.

Understandably, most of us do not want to take unnecessary risks that could leave us jobless or hit by a huge financial loss. Any decision that ignores the advice of financial experts and respected economists certainly *seems* like it would be risky. But we'll say it again: It is precisely when you blindly follow such "expert advice" that you risk hurtling over the cliff if a turning point occurs. On the other hand, if you break from the pack early enough—as soon as your dashboard warns of danger—you will *not* be acting rashly. You will be making an educated decision based on decades of research from the leaders in the field of business cycle forecasting. And, despite what you might think, you will not be alone. Multinational companies and major fund managers will be analyzing the same data and making similar decisions.

The discipline of our approach gives you a fighting chance. The next time the economy is about to turn, your dashboard will lead you to experience a moment of clarity, just like the one we have at ECRI each time a turn approaches. The leading indexes alert you to the changes ahead. But you will have to assess your position in light of the rising risks, and prepare to make critical decisions. When the world around you remains blind to the danger, however, it is very difficult to resist the powerful momentum pulling you along with the herd.

Keep in mind that your cyclical worldview gives you an enormous advantage over the hordes of people following misleading, outdated, or biased information. Still, taking action at the decisive moment will be more challenging than you imagine. This final chapter will prepare you for the difficulty of acting on your turning point forecast when others disagree.

TURNING POINTS AND RISK

A cyclical view of the economy reveals an order to the way the economy rises and falls, and the way the probability of recession varies over time. Although it may seem simpler to relinquish control by believing that recessions are not forecastable, the danger of a downturn does not disappear just because you put your head in the sand. In order to navigate future economic turns, you need to be aware of important shifts in the economy itself, as well as understand how risk shifts over time.

Depending on the nature of your decisions, you will need to monitor various areas of the economy. The more accurately you determine the level of risk in the sectors of the economy that affect the business, career-related, or personal decision you're considering, the more likely it will be well timed.

When should you change jobs? That choice definitely depends on the risk that unemployment will rise in the near term. Watch the Weekly Leading Index (WLI). If it's falling, steer clear of industries that are most affected by economic shifts. Should you hire more employees or increase production? Again, the WLI will lead the way. What about investment decisions? Sometimes the risk of holding stocks is high, as it was in 2000. The risk of owning bonds can also rise rapidly, as in 1994 and 1999, which marked the worst bond markets in history. The Future Inflation Gauge (FIG) is critical to investors here, warning when the inflation cycle may turn and go the other way. Your best course of action will depend on whether the economy or the inflation cycle is going to change direction soon. Clearly, if you make a timing mistake in any of these areas, it could take years to repair the damage. For those of us nearing retirement, there might not be enough time to ever recover.

Levels of risk wax and wane throughout the economic cycle. Small changes in employment, inflation, or economic growth occur all the time—but the risk of major changes remains relatively low as long as the economy remains in expansion. But if the economy is about to move from expansion to contraction, risk levels undergo a sea change. Launching a business or investing in stocks on the premise of a strong economy could turn out to be a poor decision if the economy enters recession. But you will know when a recession is coming by watching the WLI and the FIG. As soon as they move in a *pronounced*, *pervasive* and *persistent* manner, you should prepare for a turn. When the risk of a business cycle peak is low, the economy is likely to stay in an upturn. When the risk of a peak is high, there is a good chance that the economy is going to enter a downturn. Those who ignore that risk are no different from our old friend Wile E. Coyote, forever chasing the Road Runner and missing the turn before plunging into the chasm below.

Our leading indexes even allow you to evaluate the risk that a geopolitical event, a policy mistake, or an oil price spike might knock the economy into recession. Although many view such shocks as the cause of a recession, the economy's vulnerability to them rises and falls with fluctuations in the business cycle. We call the period of time in which a shock can tip the economy into recession a "window of vulnerability." When that window is firmly closed, it is difficult for external shocks to push the economy into recession. For example, in 1941, ECRI's U.S. Long Leading Index was in a clear upswing. Because of the strength in the cyclical drivers of the economy, even the horrific shock of the Pearl Harbor attack that December was not enough to cause a recession before wartime spending began to boost growth further. But if the leading indicators turn down, that window of vulnerability opens up, and any economic shock has the potential to endanger the expansion.

Our collection of leading indexes is like a roughly drawn map of the future, highlighting dangerous shoals. One word of caution: The economic dashboard will not make your decisions failsafe. Even when the leading indexes correctly warn of a turn ahead, your specific investment decisions may be wrong and your company can still stumble. For all we know, you could invest in buggy whips just as the automobile is being introduced. But the risk of being blindsided will drop dramatically if you have an idea of which way the economy is headed.

Nor can we promise you riches. The merits of our approach are measured in terms of risk reduction. It gives you the ability to avert major hazards that could crack your nest egg or zap your budget. We believe that the ability to reduce such risks is a crucial skill. But it is up to you to apply this knowledge.

FIGHTING THE TIDE

Remember how reassuring it seems when everyone agrees with you. But as previous recessions and depressions have taught us, most people's perception of risk will always fall a few steps behind—so much so that we could actually consider public opinion a *lagging* indicator.

Back in the early 1990s, most people thought the economy was mired in recession, despite the fact that an anemic recovery had already begun. Gray's Papaya, a hot dog shop on Broadway and Seventy-second Street in Manhattan, captured the tone perfectly by raising a large "Recession Special" sign months after the recession ended. It shows just how long lingering perceptions of recession can resonate with popular opinion. The residual gloom from the 1990–91 recession plagued the first President Bush during his 1992 reelection campaign. (Bill Clinton hammered away at him with his "it's the economy, stupid" refrain.) Yet the economy—unbeknownst to many—was embarking on the longest expansion in U.S. history.

As long as the economy continues in the same general direction, such a lag in perception will affect people slightly or not at all. But at turning points, the exposure to risk created by that lag can hit hard. When the economy is entering recession, most will assume the expansion is continuing. In other words, just when most think that risk is low, actual risk is spiking up.

Long after the recession is over and another expansion has begun, people remain mired in pessimism, a misperception that can cause them to miss some of the most attractive opportunities to appear in the course of a cycle. Those who use a cyclical world-view not only avoid the pain that comes from an unexpected upturn or downturn, they actually learn to profit from them. For example, Ryanair, an unconventional, low-cost European airline whose market capitalization recently surpassed those of British Airways and Lufthansa, uses the cycle to strengthen its bargaining power, timing aircraft purchases to coincide with recession[1] when aircraft manufacturers are most anxious to make a sale— one aspect of their business strategy that has clearly worked. But relatively few individuals or businesses make such well-timed decisions, because almost no one understands what is really happening in the economy around turning points.

At turning points, if you wait for general perceptions to change before you act, you will miss the boat. Making this mistake will cost you dearly. Yet the momentum of the pack will exert incredible pressure on you to do just that.

Recall, for example, a holiday party in the fall of 2000. The conversation turns toward the market. Everyone seems to know someone who became a millionaire betting on a dot.com company with a product that would change the world. You discuss various concerns like the presidential election, rising oil prices, or the unusually cold weather, but no one seems worried that their world is about to turn upside down. Confidence and optimism are nearly universal, even though you are alarmed because WLI growth has plunged to a twenty-year low and is warning of recession. None of your peers shares your concern.

At work, your company is completing the final steps of an ambitious expansion. Your supervisor feels confident that the economy will remain strong, and not one of your colleagues mentions the possibility that this assumption might be more risky than it seems. With the recent party experience fresh in your mind, it is clear that you will be viewed as a naysayer if you raise questions about the strength of the economy.

Similarly, if you were concerned about your investment portfolio because of high stock prices combined with a strong downturn in the WLI, and asked your broker to shift your money from stocks to bonds, she would have probably told you that you were crazy. In fact, she very well may have advised you do just the opposite. She would have had plenty of investment bank research to back her up, too. It is not easy to argue against this kind of expert advice. You watch TV and read the news with an eye for what others think. Financial news channels, reputable newspapers and business magazines, the Federal Reserve, and the President of the United States have all made clear statements about the future course of the economy that contradict what your economic dashboard is telling you.

Take a moment and think about the situation just outlined. It is not surprising that the momentum of the majority's view is overwhelmingly strong. After all, much like a car's rearview mirror, experts use forecasting tools that can recognize turning points only in hindsight. Furthermore, political and business leaders, not to mention Wall Street professionals and the media, have a vested interest in good news. If they were to predict a downturn, they would probably lose votes, investors, and advertising clients. Still, since most people's views are formed by such sources, few will be talking about recession or giving credence to those who do. Headlines will be optimistic. Stock price projections will be relatively healthy. Few of your friends or colleagues will feel compelled to pull their own money out of equities, hold off on major purchases, or downscale their business plans. While they're still focused on the rearview mirror, your economic dashboard will be flashing signals you cannot ignore.

These mistakes in perception will persist even after the recession actually arrives, exacerbating the pain of those who acted as if the downturn had been a mere hiccup in an otherwise endless expansion. Recall the information technology companies that kept expanding even after the recession had gained momentum. In fact, by the time the reality of recession was finally accepted by conventional wisdom, the economy was already starting to recover.

But the hangover from the excesses of the boom lingered. Even though the economy was actually growing again, talk of a double-dip recession became widespread. Businesses and individuals hid in the trenches, missing opportunities all around them.

Acting on your turning point forecasts and breaking from the pack does not make you a knee-jerk contrarian. In fact, for stretches at a time, you are likely to find yourself agreeing with the majority. In other words, in between the big cyclical turns in growth and inflation, the herd is often right, and you should join in.

The recession of 2001 was not just a financial shock but a psychological blow as well. With the illusion shattered, many lost faith in the framework they had been using to plan their futures. Suddenly, nothing was as it had seemed. Stock prices fell, with the Dow dropping 38 percent from its highs. Some respected corporate leaders like Ken Lay and Dennis Koslowski turned out to have feet of clay. Unemployment rose from 3.8 to 6.4 percent. Even our sense of physical safety felt threatened by unpredictable violence and international tensions. This new pessimism was a stark contrast to the unbridled optimism of the late-1990s boom, and just as dangerous.

Back in 1927, Wesley Mitchell described this cyclical phenomenon as an "error of pessimism" that follows on the heels of a "crisis of prosperity."[2]

The error of optimism dies in the crisis but in dying it "gives birth to an error of pessimism. This new error is born, not an infant, but a giant; for an industrial boom has necessarily been a period of strong emotional excitement, and an excited man passes from one form of excitement to another more rapidly than he passes to quiescence."

By adopting the longer-term perspective afforded by a cyclical worldview, you will realize that these emotional swings always chase after swings in the business cycle. But as the downturn recedes from memory, confidence and certainty begin to build, rising to new heights during the next boom, only to dissolve yet again in the wake of the next bust. Cycles of misguided certainty will exist as long as our judgment is colored by emotion.

Only an objective framework can protect you from the next compelling argument for the business cycle's demise. Leading indexes serve as a reality check by giving you a hard reading of all the relevant facts—not just those that support the prevailing mood or the headlines of the day.

What awaits around the next corner? A housing bust? Another recession? A new technology boom? No one can forecast the future precisely. But your personal economic dashboard of leading indexes can act as a guide to help you navigate the road ahead.

EMBRACING A CYCLICAL WORLDVIEW

When someone learns about our leading indicator approach and forecasting record (see chart on facing page), they often begin following our leading indexes closely. Still, it takes time and experience with the indexes to develop the confidence needed to challenge the prevailing wisdom that turning points cannot be predicted. We have heard from many erstwhile skeptics of our 2001 recession call who are now strong proponents of our work.

Even with the evidence we have presented, you may still need to experience a turn in the cycle while watching the indexes to develop complete confidence in our approach. Numerous times, people hurt by a surprising shift in the cycle have come to us asking about cycle forecasting. They soon develop an understanding of our methods. But often, only after they experience an accurate turning point call firsthand do they feel truly com-

ECRI's Track Record

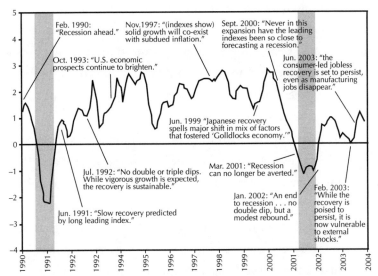

Chart showing actual ECRI forecasts since 1990 against the growth rate of ECRI's U.S. Coincident Index, which is a summary measure of economic activity. Shaded bars mark recessions.

pelled to use our approach as a vital part of their decision-making process.

With so much information available, it is natural to pick out evidence that supports what you would like to believe. It is understandable that all of us tend to favor ideological frameworks that interpret the world in a way that makes sense to us. Often this means creating a story to justify our behavior, using analysis from Wall Street, political leaders, or other pundits. There is nothing wrong with listening to these opinions, but spinning a tale based on subjective views will often lead you astray. Checking such views of the economy with the objective information offered by the leading indexes helps keep the risk of wishful thinking at bay.

As you employ the leading index approach, you will learn to cut through much of the noise and confusion present in the economic data. The objective indicators remain unaffected by emotions, vested interests, and wishful thinking, giving you the support you need to choose a different path. It might seem lonely at times, but you will have a guidebook based on an eighty-year research tradition.

Most forecasters drifted from this tradition of business cycle research long ago. As cycles became less volatile after World War II, many came to believe that this trend would continue indefinitely—and the swings in global economic activity have indeed become smaller in the last thirty years. However, having arrived at very low levels, this trend toward softer cycles may have run its course. In fact, *The Economist* bluntly concluded in a special report on business cycles that this might mark the beginning of an *era* of increased volatility.[3] In other words, turning points may now become even more frequent.

We believe that our work will aid you in navigating those turns, whatever course the economy takes. We also hope that it will foster a wider curiosity about business cycles and swing the focus of economic study back to business cycle research.

The cycles are certain. But you must watch and measure them to understand where the economy is headed in the near term. This book provides you, as a decision maker, with better tools for anticipating change. Our approach will allow you to focus on the life you want to enjoy without undue worry about every supposed twist in the economy. That is the way it should be. We live to do other things: raise children, build a business, acquire an education, travel, or develop a career. We all deserve the ability to pursue our goals in uncertain times—without being distracted by the threat of economic change.

Turning points *can* be predicted. As you lead your life and follow your dreams, use that knowledge to safeguard your future.

APPENDIX A: CRYSTAL BALLS-UP

"Forecasting is always difficult, especially when it is about the future"

The dismal scientists have a dismal record in predicting recessions. In 1929 the Harvard Economic Society reassured its subscribers days after the crash that: "A severe depression is outside the range of probability." Despite huge improvements in data and computing power, forecasters remain in the dark. In a survey in March 2001, 95% of American economists thought there would not be a recession, yet one had already started.

Why are recessions so difficult to forecast? One excuse is that economists, unlike weathermen, do not know if it is hot or cold today because their data are always out of date. They have to forecast not only the future but also the immediate past. A less good reason is that economists have a tendency to run with the pack. Predicting a recession is unpopular (especially if you work for an investment bank), and predicting one prematurely will prove costly to clients. It may also cost you your job.

Forecasts produced by economic models with hundreds of equations are notoriously bad at predicting recessions because they tend to extrapolate the recent past. This leads to big forecasting errors near turning-points, because recessions are caused by abrupt changes in the behaviour of firms and consumers. A more reliable way to spot a coming downturn is to scrutinise indicators that have given warning signals in the past. Financial indicators have the longest lead times, but a gauge that performs well in one period may do badly in another. An inverted yield curve (meaning that short-term interest rates have risen above long-term rates) has traditionally been one of the best predictors of recession. But ahead of America's 1990–91 recession the yield curve did not properly invert.

Stockmarkets are another favourite bellweather. But Paul Samuelson, a Nobel prize-winner in economics, famously quipped that the market had predicted nine of the past five recessions. In 1987, for instance, the stock-market wrongly signalled a recession in America and Europe. Few economists believe that the recent market slide signals a further recession. Leading indicators that combine several economic and financial measures seem more promising. The index of leading economic indicators (LEI), originally produced by America's Department of Commerce and now by the privately run Conference Board, is a weighted average of indicators such as share prices, interest-rate spreads, consumer confidence and new orders. Unfortunately, the LEI failed to predict any of the past three recessions.

The Economic Cycle Research Institute, a private research group, has been more successful. It was set up by the late Geoffrey Moore, a pioneer of research into business cycles. ECRI believes that turning-points can be systematically predicted. It tracks no fewer than 14 leading indices for different parts of the economy and with different lead times. ECRI was one of the few firms to forecast both of the past two American recessions. Its leading indicators for other economies have also fared well. It successfully forecast recessions in Japan in 1997 and 2001. Encouragingly, as this survey went to press ECRI was saying there was no risk of a double dip in America.

From *The Economist*, September 28–October 4, 2002

Period	Peak or Trough	United States	Canada	Mexico	Germany	France	United Kingdom	Italy	Spain	Switzerland	Sweden	Austria
1948–1950	P	11/48										
1948–1950	T	10/49										
1951–1952	P						8/52					
1951–1952	T											
1953–1955	P	7/53	5/53									
1953–1955	T	5/54	6/54									
1956–1959	P	8/57	10/56			11/57						
1956–1959	T	4/58	2/58			4/59						
1960–1961	P	4/60										
1960–1961	T	2/61										
1962–1966	P				3/66			1/64				
1962–1966	T							3/65				
1967–1968	P				5/67							
1967–1968	T											
1969–1973	P	12/69						10/70			10/70	
1969–1973	T	11/70						8/71			11/71	
1973–1975	P	11/73			8/73	7/74	9/74	4/74		4/74		8/74
1973–1975	T	3/75			7/75	6/75	8/75	4/75			7/75	6/75
1976–1978	P									3/76	11/77	
1976–1978	T											
1979–1980	P	1/80			1/80	8/79	6/79	5/80	3/80		2/80	2/80
1979–1980	T	7/80				6/80						
1981–1983	P	7/81	4/81	3/82	10/82	4/82	5/81			9/81		1/83
1981–1983	T	11/82	11/82	7/83				5/83		11/82	6/83	
1984–1986	P			10/85		12/84			5/84			
1984–1986	T			11/86								
1986–1989	P											
1986–1989	T											
1990–1991	P	7/90	3/90		1/91		5/90		11/91	3/90	6/90	
1990–1991	T	3/91										
1992–1994	P		3/92	10/92		2/92	3/92	2/92		9/93	7/93	4/92
1992–1994	T			10/93	4/94	8/93		10/93	12/93	12/94		6/93
1994–1997	P			11/94								5/95
1994–1997	T			7/95						9/96		3/96
1997–1999	P											
1997–1999	T											
2000–2001	P	3/01		8/00	1/01					3/01		1/01
2000–2001	T	11/01										12/01

	Peak or Trough	Asia Pacific							Africa	Middle East
Period		Japan	China*	India	Korea	Australia	Taiwan	New Zealand	South Africa	Jordan
1948–1950	P									
	T									
1951–1952	P					6/51				
	T					9/52				
1953–1955	P									
	T	12/54				12/55				
1956–1959	P					8/56				
	T									
1960–1961	P					12/60				
	T					9/61				
1962–1966	P			11/64				6/66		
	T			11/65						
1967–1968	P			4/66						
	T			4/67				3/68		
1969–1973	P			6/72						
	T			5/73						
1973–1975	P	11/73				6/74	12/73	4/74		
	T	2/75				1/75	1/75	3/75		
1976–1978	P							3/77	6/76	
	T							3/78	11/77	
1979–1980	P			4/79	3/79					
	T			3/80	10/80					
1981–1983	P							4/82	11/81	
	T							5/83	1/83	
1984–1986	P							11/84	6/84	
	T							3/86	2/86	
1986–1989	P							9/86		11/87
	T								2/89	
1990–1991	P			3/91		6/90				
	T			9/91		12/91		6/91		2/91
1992–1994	P	4/92							8/92	
	T	2/94								
1994–1997	P			5/96						
	T			2/97						11/95
1997–1999	P	3/97			8/97			10/97	4/97	
	T	7/99			7/98			5/98	11/98	
2000–2001	P	8/00					8/00			
	T						9/01			

SOURCE: Economic Cycle Research Institute (ECRI), New York City (except for the United States, National Bureau of Economic Research).
NOTE: Shaded cells represent periods for which data are not available.
*During the period for which data are available (1984–present), the Chinese economy experienced no business cycle recessions.
For the full updated list of Business Cycle and Growth Rate Cycle Peak and Trough Dates, please visit our website, www.businesscycle.com/research/intlcycledates.php.

NOTES

Chapter 1 • The Resurrection of Risk

1. Loungani, P. (2001), "How Accurate Are Private Sector Forecasts? Cross-Country Evidence from *Consensus Forecasts* of Output Growth," *International Journal of Forecasting,* 17 (3), 419–32.

2. "A Crystal Balls-Up" (2002), in "A Survey of the World Economy," *The Economist,* September 28.

3. *U.S. Cyclical Outlook,* Vol. V, No. 9, September 2000.

4. Leonhardt, D. (2001), "Is the Fed's Action Just in Time or Too Late?" *The New York Times,* April 19, page A1.

5. Announcement made by Business Cycle Dating Committee, National Bureau of Economic Research, on November 26, 2001. According to the classical definition, a recession is not just a fall in GDP, but a pronounced, pervasive, and persistent decline in output, income, employment, and sales. The membership of the dating committee has changed significantly in recent years, with some members suggesting that the historical recession dates should be revised, based solely or mostly on GDP. This would be a mistake, in our opinion, because a recession truly occurs when a decline, however initiated or instigated, occurs in some measure of aggregate economic activity and causes cascading declines in the other key measures of activity.

For example, when a dip in sales causes a drop in production—triggering declines in employment and income, which in turn feed back into a further sales decline—a vicious cycle results, and a recession ensues. This domino effect of weakness in one measure cascading into weakness in all of these key measures is what characterizes a recessionary downturn. At some point, the vicious cycle is broken and an analogous self-reinforcing virtuous cycle begins (see discussion and chart on pages 70–72), with increases in output, employment, income, and sales feeding into each other—the hallmark of a business cycle recovery.

The points of transition between the vicious and virtuous cycles should mark the start and end dates of recessions. Therefore, it is logical to base the choice of recession start and end dates not on any one statistic alone (such as GDP), but on the consensus of the dates when output, income, employment, and sales reach their respective turning points. This is the tried and true method ECRI uses to determine the international business cycle chronologies (Appendix B), and to deviate from this sophisticated understanding would oversimplify the complex phenomenon known as the business cycle.

6. See chart, Chapter 10, page 183.

7. "A Crystal Balls-Up" (2002), in "A Survey of the World Economy," *The Economist*, September 28.

8. Moore, G.H. (1950), *Statistical Indicators of Cyclical Revivals and Recessions*, New York: National Bureau of Economic Research.

Chapter 2 • A History of Cycles

1. Jevons, W.S. (1884), "Solar Periods and the Price of Corn," in *Investigations in Currency and Finance*, London: Macmillan.

2. Jevons, H.S. (1910), *The Causes of Unemployment, The Sun's Heat and Trade Activity*, London.

3. Moore, H.L. (1914), *Economic Cycles: Their Law and Cause*, New York: Macmillan.

4. Zahorchak, M. (1983), *Climate: The Key to Understanding Business Cycles*, Linden, NJ: Tide Press.

5. Mills, J. (1867), "Credit Cycles and the Origin of Commercial Panics," *Transactions of the Manchester Society*.

6. Pigou, A.C. (1927), *Industrial Fluctuations*, London: Macmillan.

7. Schumpeter, J.A. (1939), *Business Cycles*, New York: McGraw-Hill.

8. Mitchell, W.C. (1927), *Business Cycles: The Problem and Its Setting*, New York: NBER.

9. Mitchell, W.C., and A.F. Burns (1938), "Statistical Indicators of Cyclical Revivals," Bulletin 69, New York: NBER, May 28.

10. Conan Doyle, A. (1891), "A Scandal in Bohemia," *The Strand Magazine*.

11. Martin, J. (2000), *Greenspan: The Man Behind the Money*, Cambridge, MA: Perseus Publishing.

12. Moore, G.H. and J. Shiskin (1967), *Indicators of Business Expansions and Contractions*, New York: NBER.

13. ECRI data are updated at businesscycle.com and are also regularly covered by major newswires, including Reuters, Bloomberg, and Dow Jones.

14. Subscription information is available at businesscycle.com. For individuals, a free trial subscription is also available at businesscycle.com/freetrial.

Chapter 3 • Why the Economy Rises and Falls

1. Mack, R.P. (1956), *Consumption and Business Fluctuations: A Case Study of the Shoe, Leather, Hide Sequence*, New York: NBER.

Chapter 4 • The Boom and Bust of the 1990s

1. Glassman, J., and K. Hassett (1999), "Dow 36,000: The New Strategy for Benefiting from the Coming Rise in the Stock Market," New York: Times Books.

2. Rich, R.W., and D. Rissmiller (2001), "Understanding the Recent Behavior of U.S. Inflation," *Current Issues in Economics and Finance* 6(8), July.

3. Cecchetti, S. (2001), "Halfway to Vanquishing Volatility," *Financial Times*, August 22.

Chapter 5 • Turning Points and Leading Indicators

1. Moore, G.H. (1958), "Forecasting Industrial Production—A Comment," *Journal of Political Economy*, February.

2. Barta, P., "Indexes Disagree on Odds for Recession: Conference Board Sees Slowing, ECRI Calls R-Word 'Unavoidable,'" *The Wall Street Journal*, April 19, 2001, page A2.

Chapter 6 • Our International Experience

1. Moore, G.H., and J.P. Cullity (1994), "The Historical Record of Leading Indicators—An Answer to 'Measurement Without Theory,'" in K. H. Oppenlander and G. Poser (Eds.), *The Explanatory Power of Business Cycle Surveys*, Aldershot: Avebury.

Chapter 7 • Measuring Business Cycles: The State of the Art

1. Dua, P. and A. Banerji (2001), "A Leading Index for India's Exports," Development Research Group Study No. 23, Reserve Bank of India, Mumbai.

2. The WLI is available at businesscycle.com and also from *BusinessWeek* online.

3. Details at minerals.usgs.gov/minerals/pubs/mii.

4. Hearing before the Subcommittee on Economic Growth and Credit Formation of the Committee on Banking, Finance, and Urban Affairs, House of Representatives, One Hundred and Third Congress, Second Session, February 22, 1994.

5. Martin, J. (2000), *Greenspan: The Man Behind Money*, Cambridge, MA: Perseus Publishing, page 26.

Chapter 8 • How to Read the Economic Indicators

1. Sperling, G. (2003), "The Insider's Guide to Economic Forecasting," *Inc.*, August, page 96.

Chapter 10 • The Discipline of a Cyclical Approach

1. Bowley, G. (2003), "How Low Can You Go?" *Financial Times*, June 20.

2. Mitchell, W.C. (1927), *Business Cycles: The Problem and Its Setting*, New York: NBER, quoting A.C. Pigou.

3. "After the Bubbles," (2002), *The Economist*, September 28, page 26.

INDEX

LAKSHMAN ACUTHAN is the managing director of the Economic Cycle Research Institute (ECRI). He began working with his mentor, Geoffrey H. Moore in 1990 at Columbia University. In 1996 he helped Moore found ECRI in order to preserve and advance business cycle research and forecasting.

Achuthan plays a key role in helping asset managers, corporate strategists and government policy-makers regularly use cyclical forecasts in their decision making process. He is also the managing editor of ECRI's publications, including *U.S. Cyclical Outlook and International Cyclical Outlook*.

A frequent speaker on business cycle forecasting at universities and conferences in North America and Europe, Achuthan enjoys teaching others about the powerful applications of cyclical forecasting. He also regularly participates in a wide range of economic discussions on international television, radio, and in the financial press. He is a member of *Time* magazine's board of economists, the New York City Economic Advisory Panel, and is the Treasurer of the Downtown Economists Club. He has a B.S. in economics and a M.B.A. in international business. He is married and lives in New York City.

ANIRVAN BANERJI is the Director of Research of the Economic Cycle Research Institute, or ECRI, which he helped his mentor, Geoffrey H. Moore, establish in 1996 to preserve and promote business cycle research. From ECRI's inception until 2000, he served as Co-Director of Research with Moore, creating many leading indexes including the *Weekly Leading Index, Future Inflation Gauge* and the *JoC-ECRI Industrial Price Index*. Before that, for over a decade, he worked closely with Moore at Columbia University.

Educated at the Indian Institute of Technology, Kharagpur, the Indian Institute of Management, Ahmedabad, and Columbia University, Banerji has published articles in academic journals ranging from the *International Journal of Forecasting* to *Applied Economics* and *Management Science*. He has advised the Asian Development Bank, as well as central banks around the world, on business cycle analysis for policy making. He has also been quoted widely in the press, from *The New York Times* to *The Economist,* and has often been interviewed on international radio and television, from *CNBC* and *NPR* to *BBC* and *China Radio International*. Banerji is a member of the OECD Expert Group on Leading Indicators, and is Forecast Chair of the Forecasters Club of New York. He also serves on New York City's Economic Advisory Panel.

FREE TRIAL SUBSCRIPTION

Thank you for your interest in *Beating the Business Cycle*, and in the work of the Economic Cycle Research Institute. As a special courtesy for readers of this book, ECRI is offering a three-month free trial subscription to *Recession-Recovery Watch*, a service that is normally available on a subscription basis. This report is specifically geared to both the needs of small businesses and individuals.

While the basic updates of the Weekly Leading Index (WLI) and Future Inflation Gauge (FIG) are available without charge on our website, with this offer, readers of *Beating the Business Cycle* will be given access to exclusive WLI and FIG charts and data. *Recession-Recovery Watch* provides an advance peek at the WLI data before it is publicly released. It also monitors the Leading Home Price Index discussed on page 111 of this book.

For more details, and to activate your trial subscription, please visit businesscycle.com/freetrial. You will be asked to enter the following access code: (RECREC), which will grant you three months of free access to *Recession-Recovery Watch*.